MANAGING SOCIALISM

Managing Socialism

FROM OLD CADRES TO NEW PROFESSIONALS IN REVOLUTIONARY CUBA

HD
8038
C9
F58
1990
West

Frank T. Fitzgerald

PRAEGER

New York
Westport, Connecticut
London

Copyright Acknowledgments

The author and publisher are grateful to the following for allowing the use of excerpts from:

Fidel Castro. *Fidel Castro Speeches Vol. 2: Our Power is that of the Working People.* New York: Pathfinder Press, 1983. Reprinted by permission of Pathfinder Press. Copyright © 1983 by Pathfinder Press.

Frank Fitzgerald. ''The Reform of the Cuban Economy, 1976–1986: Organisation, Incentives and Patterns of Behaviour.'' In *Journal of Latin American Studies*. London: Cambridge University Press, 1989.

Library of Congress Cataloging-in-Publication Data

Fitzgerald, Frank T.
   Managing socialism : from old cadres to new professionals in
revolutionary Cuba / Frank T. Fitzgerald.
     p.   cm.
   Includes bibliographical references.
   ISBN 0–275–93414–4 (alk. paper)
   1. Professional employees—Cuba. 2. Professional employees—Cuba—
Political activity. 3. Elite (Social sciences)—Cuba. 4. Politics
and education—Cuba. 5. Cuba—Politics and government—1959–
I. Title.
HD8038.C9F58 1990
331.25′92′097291—dc20   89–77246

Copyright © 1990 by Frank T. Fitzgerald

All rights reserved. No portion of this book may be
reproduced, by any process or technique, without the
express written consent of the publisher.

Library of Congress Catalog Card Number: 89–77246
ISBN: 0–275–93414–4

First published in 1990

Praeger Publishers, One Madison Avenue, New York, NY 10010
An imprint of Greenwood Publishing Group, Inc.

Printed in the United States of America

The paper used in this book complies with the
Permanent Paper Standard issued by the National
Information Standards Organization (Z39.48–1984).

10 9 8 7 6 5 4 3 2 1

To my parents,
Ted and Alice Fitzgerald;

my children,
Sean and Laurie Fitzgerald;

and my compañera,
Pamela Robert;

each for very special reasons.

Contents

Tables

Preface

I first became interested in the Cuban Revolution during the 1960s, when it appeared to shine as a beacon for many of us who hoped and worked for a just society. But my interest did not turn to serious investigation until the mid–1970s. In 1975, I began reading the Cuban studies literature and following the Cuban press. Out of this effort came a first article that critiqued the notion, then gaining ground in Cuban studies, that Cuba after 1970 was going through a process of wholesale "Sovietization."[1] The encouraging reception given this article spurred me to dig deeper into the Cuban reality.

In the late 1970s, Professor James Petras of the State University of New York at Binghamton, with whom I was just beginning to work out a dissertation topic, commented that studies of the politics of the Cuban revolutionary process never moved much beyond analyzing the revolutionary leadership's policies and their apparent results. He asked if I could write an analysis that would reach below the leadership to illuminate what was happening at the intermediate level of Cuban society. I pondered this question for a long time: Given the sort of information available about Cuba and likely to be found by visiting the island, I was no more sure than he was that such an analysis was possible. To get my bearings I immersed myself in the literature of political analysis on Eastern Europe and the Soviet Union. Through this process I began to see how I might analytically structure my work to move beyond the limits of Cuban studies. However, I still worried whether the requisite information was available.

In the early 1980s, I went through various collections of Cuban documents and periodicals in the United States, and travelled to Cuba to
conduct a series of wide-ranging informal interviews. By 1983, although
still aware of the information gaps that remained, I had most of the
information I needed, and had figured out how to fill certain gaps by
constructing estimated data series. I had also identified the types of intermediate-level actors that seemed most salient and developed a perspective for analyzing them.[2]

I completed my dissertation in early 1985. Shortly thereafter, a crisis
of sorts erupted in Cuba. This produced new information, which clarified
much of what had been going on in the first half of the 1980s. This new
material added force to my argument and clearly showed the value of the
analytical perspective I had developed. I proceeded to revise and update
the whole text. The result is this book.

This work draws on a variety of social science disciplines. Yet, since
it focuses on the relationship between social stratification and politics
broadly conceived, it is essentially a work of political sociology. This
study examines major changes at the intermediate level of Cuban society,
which have been brought about by and have in turn influenced the Cuban
revolutionary process. Specifically, it focuses on the rise and decline of
different types of intermediate-level actors and on patterns of conflict and
cooperation between these and both the revolutionary leadership and
workers. First, it examines Cuba's poor skill profile in the early years of
the revolution, which arose in part from the exodus of a portion of the
country's prerevolutionary intermediate strata. Second, it explores the
conditions that spurred the rise and subsequent decline of what I call the
"old cadres," who in the 1960s rose to intermediate-level occupations
on the basis of political rather than educational qualifications. Third, it
analyzes the emergence of what I call the "new professionals," who
largely after 1970 entered these same types of occupations on the basis
of educational credentials and presumed expertise.

A major concern of this study is to understand the formation and rise
of the new professionals and their interactions with other sets of Cuban
actors. Rapidly expanding in the 1970s, and especially after 1975, the
new professionals are now quite numerous and continue to increase. More
and more the new professionals occupy critical intermediate-level positions in Cuban society and are becoming an important sociopolitical force
in the Cuban revolutionary process. Although these new intermediate
actors have so far been largely ignored by Cuba scholars,[3] as this study
will attempt to demonstrate, it is no longer possible to comprehend ad-

equately the contours of stratification or the conflicts of politics in Cuba without recognizing the importance of the new professionals.

A work of this sort is more a community than an individual product. Although I take individual responsibility for everything in this book, I am keenly aware that through this whole process I have been at the center of a network of generous support. Therefore, I gladly thank Professor James F. Petras for suggesting the topic of this book: His critical insights, encouragement, and friendship have helped keep me going throughout this project. Without the deft intervention of Professor Terence K. Hopkins, institutional support for this project might have disappeared. Also, I must thank him and Professor Melvin Leiman for stimulating my awareness about the broader implications of this study. Useful comments were also made by Linda Fuller and Art MacEwan.

I thank those colleagues at the College of Saint Rose who have encouraged my scholarly endeavors for many years, and especially Donald Tappa, former academic vice president, for the financial support he provided through his office. For reading and commenting upon parts of this study at various stages, I thank my Saint Rose colleagues Carl Swidorski, Keith Haynes, and Richard P. Wunderlich. For moral support, I thank Honora Kinney and Karin Welsh. For diligently reading the whole text several times, and helping improve the quality and readability of my analysis, I thank Professor Malcolm Willison.

My good friend Stephen Price, who kept me on target through the early stages of this project, deserves thanks not only for giving so generously of his time, but for doing so with good humor and bad jokes; they cheered me on through many a day at the typewriter. Both Chris Anastasio and Bob Mitchell were key to the completion of this project. The one taught me how to relax by sinking an eight ball, the other how to keep from getting stuck behind one. I thank Pamela Robert for her encouraging words whenever my spirits flagged, and for generously providing me with the emotional atmosphere that helped me complete this work; she knows I am deeply indebted to her for far more than I can possibly enumerate here.

This study could not have been carried out without the help of the many *compañeros* and *compañeras* in Cuba, who were willing to engage in long and, for me, fruitful discussions. Nor could it have been completed without the aid of the many librarians at the College of Saint Rose, State University of New York at Albany, University of Massachusetts at Amherst, University of Pittsburgh, United Nations, and Center for Cuban Studies, who found what I needed, even when I was not sure what that was. I thank them all. Finally, thanks to Darby Penney, Mary Lou McDonald, and Clara Winans for typing parts of this text, and to Nabeel Khoury and Conrad Crasto for introducing me to the word processor.

NOTES

1. Frank T. Fitzgerald, "A Critique of the 'Sovietization of Cuba' Thesis," *Science and Society* 42 (Spring 1978), pp. 1–32; for an update, see Frank T. Fitzgerald, "The 'Sovietization of Cuba Thesis' Revisited," in Andrew Zimbalist, ed., *Cuban Political Economy: Controversies and Cubanology* (Boulder, Colorado: Westview Press, 1988), pp. 137–53, and in *Science and Society*, 51, 4 (Winter 1987–1988), pp. 439–57.

2. Frank T. Fitzgerald, "Politics and Social Structure in Revolutionary Cuba: From the Demise of the Old Middle Class to the Rise of the New Professionals" (Ph.D. diss., State University of New York at Binghamton, 1985).

3. A notable exception is Sergio Roca, "State Enterprises in Cuba under the New System of Planning and Management (SDPE)," *Cuban Studies/Estudios Cubanos* 16 (1986), which discusses enterprise managers. As will be seen further on, however, Roca's perception of the relationship between enterprise managers and their superordinates is distorted by the elite/mass perspective he shares with many Cuba scholars. See also the largely descriptive study by the Cuban Francisco Ferreira Báez, "El sistema de formación profesional de nivel medio en Cuba," in Haydée García and Hans Blumenthal, eds., *Formación Profesional en Latinoamerica* (Caracas: Editorial Nueva Sociedad, 1987), pp. 111–38.

1

Introduction: Cuban Studies and the Analysis of Socialist Societies

Research on revolutionary Cuba has advanced markedly over the past two decades. As more and better information has become available, the number of scholars working on Cuba and of issues addressed and debated has increased. Analytically, however, Cuban studies has remained at a low level of sophistication. Despite an increasing number of dissenting voices,[1] Cuban studies continues to be dominated by scholars whose understanding of the politics of the Cuban revolutionary process has been limited by a narrowly focused and often highly speculative analytic approach. To advance further, Cuban studies must break through these analytic limits.

THE LIMITS OF CUBAN STUDIES

Like their counterparts in East European and Soviet studies who have viewed these societies as totalitarian,[2] the leading Cuba scholars have failed to move beyond the notion that Cuban society is dominated by an all-powerful, and therefore politically salient, elite that imposes whatever policies it wants on a powerless, and therefore politically irrelevant, mass. These scholars have focused their attention disproportionately on revolutionary Cuba's top leaders, and have largely ignored the intermediate and lower levels of Cuban society. In part, this may be the result of their tailoring theory to the most readily available types of information. But it also stems from the dominance of the elite/mass perspective itself. This perspective, and the distortions to which it leads, can be seen most clearly in the big books, offering overall interpretations of the direction and shape of Cuban society, that have been written since 1970.

In his widely influential *Cuba in the 1970s*,[3] for example, Carmelo Mesa-Lago argued that after 1970 Cuba underwent a process of wholesale "Sovietization." As he put it: "The uniqueness of the Cuban revolution . . . has gradually dulled and the more conventional features of socialism 'à la Eastern Europe' appear increasingly stronger on the island."[4] Among these features Mesa-Lago counted the return to material incentives and wage differentials to spur productivity and the imposition of Soviet-style economic and political institutions. These latter, he claimed, were characterized by "central controls, dogmatism, administrative and bureaucratic features, and limited mass participation resembling the Soviet system."[5] He saw all of these changes, moreover, as brought about by a Cuban elite increasingly dependent economically on the Soviet bloc and, therefore, increasingly responsive to Soviet pressure.

The interested reader can find my critique of the Sovietization thesis elsewhere.[6] Mesa-Lago's elite/mass perspective is all that is relevant here, and I want simply to point out one of the typical distortions that has resulted from it. Intent upon seeing the post–1970 reemphasis on personal material incentives as an elite imposition, Mesa-Lago characterized these mechanisms as simply a "managerial tool for the control of labor productivity."[7] What this characterization ignored, besides the long-term interest of workers in expanded production, was that the new incentive system helped protect workers from administrative waste and misuse of labor. The new incentive system ensured workers overtime pay for any extra work necessitated by administrative errors and inefficiency. The new system therefore served as a clear disincentive for the administrative practices of wasting and hoarding labor that had been rampant in the 1960s, and about which workers had loudly complained. In short, Mesa-Lago's elite/mass perspective blinded him to the complexity of the social interests involved in the incentive question.

Jorge Domínguez also put forth an elite/mass perspective, as well as the Sovietization thesis, in his *Cuba: Order and Revolution*.[8] The careful reader of this massive book is often jolted by contradictions between its specific findings and its overall perspective. Perhaps the most dramatic instance is Domínguez's analysis of what he calls the strike of 1970. This refers to the dramatic rise in worker absenteeism and fall in worker productivity, as the revolutionary leadership attempted to mobilize the whole population to produce 10 million tons of sugar in 1970. To call this a strike overstates the political and organizational cohesion of the workers involved, but Domínguez was certainly right: "This protest is important because it shows that the power of the central leadership in Cuba has its limits.''[9] The problem is that Domínguez failed to explain how this insight did not contrast with his overall elite/mass perspective; the reader is left to decide how this and other contradictions that pepper Domínguez's book might be resolved. At no point did he attempt to discuss the basis and extent of working class power in Cuba. His elite/mass perspective seems to have prevented him from acknowledging theoretically what his empirical investigation brought to light.

If his elite/mass perspective at times led Domínguez to overlook the broader significance of his specific findings, at other times it rendered his interpretations tendentious. For example, in one place he stated:

The difficulty in getting some sense of public mood without opening the entire system up to criticism may explain why so much stress is placed on participation through technical means like surveys. These measures gather information without threatening local officials and without risking any expression of coordinated opposition to national politics at the local level.[10]

This statement refers to the sociological surveys that organizations such as the Institute of Internal Demand have increasingly utilized since 1970. This institute has used surveys to gather information, for example, on the existing stock of household furnishings, the type of work clothes and uniforms desired by particular occupational groups, and consumer items most desired by the population. Yet despite their obvious content, Domínguez interprets such surveys as mechanisms for gathering data while avoiding genuine political participation because he will not step outside his elite/mass perspective.[11]

In the study of East European and Soviet systems, the totalitarian interpretation eventually came under attack from interest group analysts seeking to widen the focus of analytic attention to include intermediate-level actors among the politically relevant actors.[12] When Cuba scholars have tried their hand at interest group analysis, however, they have typically done so still within the confines of an elite/mass perspective. The only interest groups that Cuba scholars have generally focused on have been factions within the elite itself, which they have commonly defined as the members of the Central Committee of the Communist Party. Consistent with their totalitarian interpretation, Cuba scholars have typically narrowed interest group analysis to the study of elite factions.

In addition, unlike interest group analysts in East European and Soviet studies, Cuba scholars have typically ignored David Truman's fundamental distinction between categoric and interest groups. Truman, an early formulator of so-called group theory, defined a categoric group as "any collection of individuals who have some characteristic in common."[13] By contrast, he defined an interest group in terms of a set of shared attitudes, and he specifically warned against imputing "an interest to a group on an *a priori* basis that may bear no relation to the attitudes held by the group."[14] In other words, Truman insisted that whether a categoric group constituted an interest group had to be established with empirical evidence.

An interest group analysis operating with Truman's distinction, of course, could legitimately proceed in either of two directions. One could identify a categoric group and then search for the shared attitudes that would prove that it was also an interest group. Or one could begin by identifying a set of shared attitudes and then seek the categoric group sharing them to prove that it constituted an interest group. In their formative work designed to establish the relevance of interest group analysis for socialist societies, H. Gordon Skilling and Franklin Griffiths utilized the first procedure.[15] The second approach has been commonly utilized by scholars concerned with identifying which groups support the various sides of a public issue.[16] But regardless of the direction of analysis, categoric and interest groups must be connected with evidence.

Because they have ignored Truman's quite simple and obvious distinction and its proper application, Cuba scholars have produced interest group analyses marred by a priori speculation. As an indication of this, Cuba scholars have had enormous difficulty identifying the salient elite factions. Different analysts, for example, have posited cleavages between *fidelista* and *raúlista* loyalists,[17] between Party and government officials,[18] between "old" and "new" Communists,[19] and between military and civilian leaders.[20] If the Cuban leadership were so factionalized, one would have to wonder how it ever promulgated or implemented any consistent policy at all. In fact, however, by failing to empirically establish that their categoric groups were also interest groups in Truman's sense, Cuba scholars have not demonstrated the divisiveness of the Cuban leadership but merely the truth of Mary McAuley's sardonic observation: "the interest group analyst inevitably finds *his* interest groups."[21]

In a typical study, Edward González identified individuals who in 1959 had been members of the July 26 Movement, whom he called *fidelistas*, and those of the Popular Socialist Party (PSP), whom he called old Communists, as the relevant interest groups or elite factions within the Cuban political system of 1975.[22] He picked out these groups because they played different roles in the overthrow of Batista, because they presumably enjoyed a different relationship with the Soviet leadership, and because they had come into open conflict with one another in 1962 and in 1968 over the machinations of ex-PSP Executive Secretary Anibal Escalante. González noted that, in 1965 when these and other groups combined to form the new Cuban Communist Party, the *fidelistas* took all seats in the Political Bureau and most in the Central Committee. After the First Party Congress was held in 1975, the *fidelistas* maintained their majority, but the old Communists increased their number of seats in these higher bodies. It was on this relative shift that González attempted to ground his interpretation of Cuban politics in the mid–1970s.

The question of whether González accurately identified the most salient elite interest groups of the early revolutionary process cannot be examined here.[23] More germane to the purpose at hand is the question of whether the presumed *fidelista*/old Communist split of the early years remained relevant in the mid–1970s. The claim that these past organizational affiliations were still important required some justification. Yet absent from González's analysis was any attempt to demonstrate that significant policy rifts still separated his designated "interest groups." The best he could do was to speculate that the rise of the old Communists was an expression of Cuba's post–1970 accommodation with the Soviet Union, and that, as a result of *fidelistas* and old Communists sharing power, "Cuban policy ... may well become more volatile in the future."[24] With this latter remark, González put off until the indefinite future the central question of his analysis, namely, whether demonstrable policy differences existed between his designated groups, and therefore whether these were truly interest rather than just categoric groups.

In another study, William LeoGrande investigated the representation of Party, government, and military personnel on the Central Committee between 1965 and 1975.[25] Among other things, he found that over this period military representation dropped, while Party and government representation rose. From this, LeoGrande concluded that

the most important elite cleavage in Cuba appears to be institutionally based. The composition of the political elite in the 1960s clearly and accurately reflected the relative strengths of the various political institutions. . . . The changing composition of the elite also indicates that there has been an important realignment . . . of institutional influence.[26]

Certainly, LeoGrande pointed out an important change in institutional representation on the Central Committee. The conclusions he drew from this change, however, were purely speculative. He offered no evidence to buttress his implicit assumption that all institutional groups were interested in the greatest possible Central Committee representation, and he failed to address the equally plausible possibility that a significant portion of the military leadership might consider involvement in the political realm a harmful distraction from their organization's proper role. Even more important, LeoGrande neither found nor looked for any policy disagreement that would justify calling the military/civilian distinction "the most important elite cleavage in Cuba." He simply stated, rather than demonstrated, that his categoric groups constituted interest groups.

In some of his recent work, Sergio Roca has departed from the pattern of sheer speculation on possible leadership factions in Cuba.[27] Through interviews with administrative and technical personnel who left Cuba between 1978 and 1981, Roca has begun to focus analytic attention on the intermediate level of Cuban society. Despite this advance, however, he has not entirely escaped the elite/mass perspective. For, as his analysis made clear, he assumed that in Cuba influence always flows down from the top and never up from the intermediate or lower levels. He discussed many instances of what I will call bureaucratic centralism, in which top-level bodies interfere with the responsibilities of lower-level bodies. But he noted bureaucratic centralism only when it was malign, only when it immediately harmed those at the intermediate level. He entirely missed the existence of benign bureaucratic centralism, where top-level bodies interfere to help those at the intermediate level. He missed this, I think, because benign bureaucratic centralism often comes in response to pressure from below, which his elite/mass perspective prevented him from recognizing. By failing to fully jettison the elite/mass perspective, Roca, like other leading Cuba scholars, failed to see the complexities of Cuban reality.

In sum, the predominant approach in Cuban studies has failed to advance beyond the elite/mass perspective, reminiscent of the totalitarian approach in East European and Soviet studies. In addition, Cuba scholars have typically reduced interest group analysis to a speculative search for elite factions, and they have failed to utilize interest group analysis to widen the focus of analytic attention to bring intermediate-level actors into view. Even Roca's exceptional attempt to focus on the intermediate level suffered from his adherence to the elite/mass view. Given the distortions to which this view leads, there is great need to move beyond the limits of current Cuban studies.

A NEW DIRECTION FOR CUBAN STUDIES

We can begin to overcome the limits of Cuban studies by borrowing an important insight from interest group analysts of Eastern Europe and the Soviet Union. While agreeing that final policy determination rested in the hands of the top revolutionary leadership, these analysts moved beyond the totalitarian perspective by insisting that intermediate actors could and indeed necessarily did intervene "in the phase of deliberation prior to the formal making of final decisions" and again "in the period of implementing" such decisions.[28] Even if it could be shown for Cuba that intermediate actors typically had little or no say in pre-decision-making discussions, they would necessarily play an important role in post-decision-making implementation. At the very least, intermediate actors could either execute or block, expedite or delay, abide by or distort, the implementation of leadership decisions.

Although, to my knowledge, interest group analysts have never extended their insight so far, the same argument can be applied to workers, who also necessarily play a role at least in post-decision-making implementation. As the direct producers of economic goods and services, workers, in fact, possess ultimate responsibility for the successful implementation of many types of economic decisions. And like intermediate actors, workers can either cooperate with or resist decisions made elsewhere. Understanding what actually happens in socialist societies, as opposed to simply what the leadership hopes will happen, requires attending to the critical role that both intermediate actors and workers play in implementing decisions.

Moreover, except in peculiar circumstances, it would be unrealistic to expect decision-making power to be so concentrated in the hands of leaders that they alone participate in pre-decision-making discussions. Intermediate actors, for example, are likely to be called upon by leaders to participate in the pre-decision-making phase, if for no other reason than that they are likely to possess relevant information, knowledge, or skills. The degree to which these actors can actually influence leadership decisions is likely to vary widely, from issue to issue, within the same society from time to time, and from society to society. But their influence is only rarely likely to be altogether absent.

Again, the same holds for workers. In fact, there are at least two structural reasons to expect that socialist workers will commonly participate and wield some influence in pre-decision-making discussions. First, in socialist systems the line that separates the private and public spheres is radically different from what it is in capitalist systems. State ownership of the major means of production results in political and economic organizations, as well as organizational leadership groups, being less officially differentiated from one another than they are, at least formally, in capitalist systems. Therefore, what are commonly considered private economic issues under capitalism quickly become public issues in a socialist system. Issues such as wage levels, incentive systems, even utilization of the economic surplus, which under capitalism are often segregated into the private or nonpolitical sphere, are typically turned into fully political issues in socialist systems. As a result, it is difficult, if not impossible, for socialist leaders to deny their share of responsibility for unpopular economic policies or results, and even socialist workers concerned solely with "economistic" issues of wages and benefits are often brought into direct political conflict with the revolutionary leadership.[29] If workers are not allowed some degree of pre-decision-making participation, or if their expectations are not accommodated to some extent, the consequences are likely to be politically disruptive, as events in Poland since 1980, for example, have shown. Knowing this, revolutionary leaders are likely to favor some measure of worker participation, and will at least commonly take note of worker expectations in their policy calculations.

Second, socialist systems guarantee something very close to full employment. In this, they differ qualitatively from capitalist systems, which require a surfeit of labor to keep workers afraid for their jobs, and thus subservient and disciplined. This structural difference, moreover, is not simply economic but profoundly political. In socialist systems, what Max Weber once dubbed the "whip of hunger" no longer operates with full force, and productive effort must be elicited from workers through other means. Without effective mechanisms to replace the pressures of the capitalist labor market, socialist systems can be expected to face continual productivity crises, which in themselves are likely to result in political problems. The fact that revolutionary leaders cannot resort to unemployment to back up their attempt to elicit productive effort gives workers considerable political leverage. This they commonly express through noncooperation with economic goals, policies, and norms, unless they are allowed at least minimal participation in decision making.

To deal with these structural realities, revolutionary leaders have two types of choices. They can either opt for coercion—a short-run solution that always entails long-run problems—or for some combination of consumer goods, political exhortation, and worker participation. The last in part accounts for the peculiar institutional structure of socialist societies, which places great emphasis on mechanisms of mass participation. Those who scoff at such mechanisms as only ritualistic have to be asked why so much time and energy is spent on mere window dressing. Surely such mechanisms signal the need for revolutionary leaders to elicit voluntary cooperation from labor that cannot easily be kept focused on economistic demands and that is no longer threatened by the whip of hunger.

Widening the focus of analytic attention sufficiently to bring the intermediate actors and workers into view and to bestow on them some political relevance, of course, suggests a question that the leading Cuba scholars, trapped in their elite/mass perspective, have never broached. Specifically, it raises the question of what attitudes or behaviors these actors might exhibit, and what patterns of conflict and cooperation might typically exist between them and other actors. To the extent that this question has been addressed within East European and Soviet studies, opinions have varied widely. Some have posited conflict between revolutionary leaders and intermediate actors for societal hegemony.[30] Others have viewed both leaders and intermediate actors as ultimately allied against workers.[31] And still others have considered all such conflicts as secondary and contained within an overarching system of mutual interests and cooperative relations.[32] In other words, scholars have disagreed in their estimation of the most salient lines of cleavage and of the severity of the conflict likely to arise along these lines.

Of course, such questions cannot be decided for Cuba on the basis either of East European and Soviet studies or of general theoretical considerations. Although future comparative work may render some general conclusions, these are empirical questions that must first be answered on the merits of each case. To proceed otherwise would simply replicate, albeit on a different level, the speculative approach of some leading Cuba scholars. This book will attempt to avoid such speculation by grounding its analysis as fully as possible in empirical evidence.

SOURCES OF EVIDENCE

I gained much of my sense of the actors and relationships that make up the Cuban stratification system through the interviews I conducted in Cuba. But because of their necessarily informal character and nonscientific sampling, they could not be relied upon to be representative enough to serve as the primary empirical underpinning for the major themes and conclusions of this work. Cuba scholars have long been aware of the virtual impossibility of "outsiders" conducting scientific survey research in Cuba. The few who have bravely tried have come away with suggestive impressions, but admittedly less than scientific results.[33] To avoid such an outcome, I have used the interviews I conducted very selectively, mostly to add color to parts of the argument and to corroborate information gathered from other sources.

For the most part, therefore, I have relied in this work on published sources, both primary and secondary, not to compile the writings of others, but to break new ground. The topic and overall argument of this book are unique. From existing data, I have derived time series that are new. Primary sources are used throughout, and I have treated secondary sources in a primary fashion, that is, as giving "the words of the witnesses . . . of an event."[34] For example, a professional journal article written by a Cuban economist is taken, not as a work of secondary analysis, but as the direct testimony of a witness, which elucidates either the events witnessed, the perspective of the witness, or both.

Relying so heavily on published sources, of course, has definite advantages. Such sources provide testimony from only a select group of witnesses, chosen not by the researcher but by those who control the print media, but they are free of the bias that results from interaction between researcher and witness. The researcher may be led astray by such sources, but not because of any direct interaction with the witness. Perhaps most important, published sources can be checked by other scholars. Any source has the disadvantages and advantages of its type. This simply underscores the need for all sources to be used carefully and critically, as I have attempted to do throughout this book. Since most of the sources are published, interested scholars can easily evaluate my success in this regard.

TERMS AND CONCEPTS

The terms and concepts used in the social sciences are seldom innocent. At the very least, most of them carry the connotations of their origin. The social sciences have developed in an attempt to comprehend the transition from feudalism to capitalism and the subsequent trajectory of the latter, and social science terminology is filled with meanings historically associated with these processes. A danger exists, then, that by applying such terminology to later processes, such as the transition from capitalism to socialism with which this study is concerned, the new emergent reality will be distorted by too close association with the old reality and the theories constructed to explain it.

Here this problem arises most seriously with the term "professional." As Eliot Friedson has emphasized, this term has carried two very different meanings, which have often been confused.[35] In its strong sense, profession refers to a limited number of occupations that successfully develop an exclusive identity and organize to claim esoteric status for their knowledge and skills, in order to gain advantages of prestige, income, and shelter from market competition. It is profession in this strong sense that has drawn attention from sociologists concerned with the pursuit of professionalization and professional authority on the part of certain occupations in developed capitalist societies.

In its weak sense, however, profession refers to a broad stratum of quite varied intermediate-level occupations that are distinguished from other occupational strata simply by the higher level of educational achievement required of their incumbents. In Cuba, entry into these intermediate-level occupations has come to require at least a secondary school degree. In this weak sense, professions exist in all types of societies that have reached a level of economic development that requires advanced qualifications through specialized education. Although this book will touch upon the question of whether the new professionals in socialist Cuba possess the attributes of a profession in the strong sense associated with certain occupations in developed capitalist societies, we are concerned here with professions primarily in the weak sense.

In addition, the reader should note that choice of the term new professionals is somewhat arbitrary. These actors could also be called the new mental workers, new technicians, new managers, new specialists, or a variety of other names. Each of these, however, shares with new professionals the tendency to draw attention to certain characteristics and to distract attention from other aspects of the whole occupational stratum. For example, for many readers new mental workers might primarily signify individuals directly involved in production, and it might distract attention from, say, university professors. I chose new professionals in order to draw attention to the fact that these actors have entered intermediate-level occupations on the basis of presumed expertise as judged by possession of certain educational credentials.

There are several other terms that I use throughout this book, such as societal decisions, revolutionary leadership, intermediate-level occupations, and old cadres, that fortunately do not present the same difficulties as new professionals and that simply require formal definition.

By societal decisions I mean those fundamental policy decisions that determine the overall direction of the revolutionary process and the shape of the organizational structures and other mechanisms and procedures through which that process is advanced. In Cuba, these would include, among other things, the decisions to mobilize the population to produce ten million tons of sugar in 1970, to institutionalize democratic centralist forms of organization in the 1970s, and to launch a major rectification campaign in 1986.

The revolutionary leadership is that relatively small number of top-level leaders who, although they may do much else besides, make these societal decisions. Although it is clear that these leaders occupy the commanding posts of both the Party and the state in Cuba, I define them according to their function as makers of societal decisions rather than their institutional location, as is more usual. Besides the well-known key figures like Fidel Castro and a few others, very little is known about who actually participates in making societal decisions in Cuba. Specifying only members of the Political Bureau or the Council of State would perhaps omit some important figures, while including all members of the Central Committee or the National Assembly would perhaps add in some unimportant ones. The point is that, in our current state of knowledge, we have no way of knowing where to draw the line. And, until we do know, it seems prudent to use a functional, rather than a misleading institutional definition of the revolutionary leadership.

The term old cadres signifies here those incumbents of intermediate-level occupations who do not possess the secondary school degree that has become officially the minimum educational credential for these positions. Rather, they were awarded these positions during the 1960s because of their political reliability. Since the early 1970s, however, the old cadres have been gradually displaced by the new professionals, who have been entering these same occupations on the basis of their educational credentials. Thus, the old cadres and the new professionals are differentiated by their educational level, not by their occupational positions.

I use the term "intermediate-level occupations" in both the prerevolutionary and postrevolutionary periods. For the first period, the term refers to the occupations of small business proprietor, manager, technician, and professional, as given in the Cuban census of 1953. For the period after 1959, it refers to those occupations in the state, political, and mass organizations (i.e., excluding the relatively small and diminishing private sector) whose incumbents (1) do not typically participate in the making of societal decisions, (2) nor directly or predominantly in material or nonmaterial production processes, but rather (3) design, organize, or direct these processes, and oversee and coordinate the activities of other individuals in these processes.

The first and second parts of this definition distinguish the incumbents of these occupational roles from revolutionary leaders and from workers, respectively. It should be clear from the third part of this definition that what is referred to is a very broad stratum of occupations. The lower level of this stratum consists in material production of what the Cubans call medium-level technicians (*técnicos medios*), who direct and control technical processes and coordinate the activities of other workers. In the hierarchy of Cuban labor categories, these stand just above skilled workers (*obreros calificados*), who do not engage in overseeing the work of others.[36] The lower level of the intermediate stratum in nonmaterial production includes individuals, such as primary or secondary school teachers, who design, direct, and oversee the processes of those under their supervision, such as their students' learning. The higher level of the whole stratum includes individuals who perform managerial, scientific, or technical work at the central state or ministerial level, teach in a university, or do research, depending on their expertise. Of course, between these higher and lower levels fall a wide variety of other occupational slots.

It should be noted that, although the content and context commonly makes clear which is meant, current Cuban terminology obscures the distinction drawn here between old cadre and new professional incumbents of intermediate-level occupations. Cubans sometimes refer to "new professionals,"[37] but with no regularity. They as easily speak of specialists, managers, or technicians trained by the revolution. They indiscriminately call all administrative personnel "cadres,"[38] and appear to have no special term for the old cadres identified here. The fact that Cuban usage hides the distinction between old cadres and new professionals, of course, heightens the significance of its disclosure here.

OVERVIEW OF BOOK

This is a study of the relationship in revolutionary Cuba between social stratification and politics broadly conceived. Its major innovation is to widen the focus of analytic attention to identify and examine the salient actors at the intermediate level of Cuban society. In addition, it seeks to uncover typical patterns of conflict and cooperation between different types of intermediate-level actors and both the workers below them and the revolutionary leadership above them in decision-making power.

Chapter 2 examines the inadequacies of the prerevolutionary educational system, the exodus of U.S. nationals and some intermediate-level Cubans, and the policies of the revolutionary leadership. It considers their relative contribution to the scarcity, misallocation, and lack of skills that severely plagued the revolution in its early years.

Chapter 3 analyzes the early educational and organizational responses of the revolutionary leadership to this skill problem. It argues that these responses were important in engendering the political-economic crisis of 1970, which led to a variety of changes that, among other things, gave rise to the emergence of the new professionals.

Chapter 4 discusses the post–1970 rectification process. This created the supply of new professionals through educational changes and raised the demand for new professions through new democratic centralist political and economic structures.

Chapter 5 analyzes various aspects of the decline of the old cadres and the rise of the new professionals. It focuses especially on the revolutionary leadership's attempt to manage this transition after 1970.

Chapter 6 considers the problem of bureaucratic centralism and underscores typical patterns of conflict and cooperation between old cadres, new professionals, revolutionary leaders, and workers in the Cuban economy from the mid–1970s to 1986.

Chapter 7 concludes by discussing the rectification campaign that the revolutionary leadership launched in 1986. It then summarizes the major findings of the book and relates them to the issues raised in this first chapter.

The major goal of this study is to show that to comprehend what is actually happening at any particular time in Cuban society, rather than what the revolutionary leadership announces it wants to happen, requires moving beyond the elite/mass perspective. This book focuses on the creation and displacement of different types of intermediate-level actors and on their relationships with both revolutionary leaders and workers. Most important, it analyzes the rise and decline of the old cadres and the emergence of the new professionals. This book is designed to illustrate that greater understanding of the revolutionary process can be gained by widening the focus of analytic attention beyond a narrowly defined elite, by concretely demonstrating the political relevance of intermediate-level actors and workers in revolutionary Cuba.

NOTES

1. For an excellent selection of these, see Andrew Zimbalist, ed., *Cuban Political Economy: Controversies in Cubanology* (Boulder, Colorado: Westview Press, 1988).

2. See, for example, Carl G. Friedrich and Zbigniew Brzezinski, *Totalitarian Dictatorship and Autocracy* (New York: Praeger, 1956); Carl G. Friedrich et al., *Totalitarianism in Perspective* (New York: Praeger, 1969); Hannah Arendt, *The Origins of Totalitarianism* (New York: Harcourt Brace, 1966).

3. Carmelo Mesa-Lago, *Cuba in the 1970s: Pragmatism and Institutionalization* (Albuquerque: University of New Mexico Press, 1974).

4. Ibid., p. x.

5. Ibid., p. 115.

6. Frank T. Fitzgerald, "A Critique of the 'Sovietization of Cuba' Thesis," *Science and Society* 42 (Spring 1978), pp. 1–32; and "The 'Sovietization of Cuba Thesis' Revisited," in Zimbalist, ed., *Cuban Political Economy*, pp. 137–53.

7. Mesa-Lago, *Cuba*, p. 36.

8. Jorge Domínguez, *Cuba: Order and Revolution* (Cambridge: Harvard University Press, 1978).

9. Ibid., p. 276.

10. Ibid., p. 304.

11. For a study that takes the increasing use of such surveys in socialist societies elsewhere as an indication of "liberalization," see Walter D. O'Connor, *Public Opinion in European Socialist Systems* (New York: Praeger, 1977).

12. For one of the most influential criticisms and alternative perspectives, see H. Gordon Skilling and Franklin Griffiths, *Interest Groups in Soviet Politics* (Princeton: Princeton University Press, 1971).

13. David Truman, *The Governmental Process* (New York: Knopf, 1971), p. 23.

14. Ibid., pp. 63–64.

15. Skilling and Griffiths, *Interest Groups in Soviet Politics*.

16. See, for example, Theodore Friedgut, "Interests and Groups in Soviet Policy-Making: The MTS Reforms," *Soviet Studies* 28 (Oct. 1976), pp. 524–47; Walter D. O'Connor, "Social Consequences of Economic Reform in Eastern Europe," in Zbigniew M. Fallenbucki, ed., *Economic Development in the Soviet Union and Eastern Europe*, vol. 1 (New York: Praeger, 1975), pp. 65–99; Joel J. Schwartz and William R. Keech, "Group Influence and the Policy Process in the Soviet Union," *American Political Science Review* 3 (Sept. 1968), pp. 840–51; Philip Stewart, "Soviet Interest Groups and the Policy Process: The Repeal of Production Education," *World Politics* 1 (Oct. 1969), pp. 29–50.

17. Edward González, "Political Succession in Cuba," *Studies in Comparative Communism* 9 (Spring/Summer 1976), pp. 80–107; Edward González, "Complexities of Cuban Foreign Policy," *Problems of Communism* 26 (Nov.-Dec. 1977), pp. 1–15; M. L. Vellinga, "The Military and the Dynamics of the Cuban Revolution," *Comparative Politics* 8 (Jan. 1976), pp. 245–71.

18. William M. LeoGrande, "Continuity and Change in the Cuban Political Elite," *Cuban Studies/Estudios Cubanos* 8 (July 1978), pp. 1–31.

19. Edward González, "Castro and Cuba's New Orthodoxy," *Problems of Communism* 25 (Jan.-Feb. 1976), pp. 1–19; Mesa-Lago, *Cuba in the 1970s*.

20. Jorge Domínguez, "Institutionalization and Civil-Military Relations in Cuba," *Cuban Studies/Estudios Cubanos* 6 (Jan. 1976), pp. 39–65; LeoGrande, "Continuity and Change."

21. Mary McAuley, *Politics and the Soviet Union* (New York: Penguin, 1977), p. 315 (emphasis added).

22. González, "Castro and Cuba's New Orthodoxy."

23. Why is one to think, for example, that the two Escalante affairs affronted only the *fidelistas* as a group but not also a significant number of old Communists? Why, in other words, is one to think that these events indicated a cleavage between *fidelistas* and old Communists rather than a cleavage within one or both of these groups? In this regard, it is interesting to note that in exposing Escalante's activities, Fidel Castro took care not to condemn the whole PSP or even its leading members. See Fidel Castro, "Against Bureaucracy and Sectarianism," in Michael Taber, ed., *Fidel Castro Speeches: Our Power Is that of the Working People*, vol. 2 (New York: Pathfinder Press, 1983), pp. 38–67.

24. González, "Castro and Cuba's New Orthodoxy," p. 5.

25. LeoGrande, "Continuity and Change."

26. Ibid., p. 27.

27. Sergio Roca, "State Enterprises in Cuba under the New System of Planning and Management (SDPE)," *Cuban Studies/Estudios Cubanos* 16 (1986), pp. 153–79.

28. H. Gordon Skilling, "The Party, Opposition and Interest Groups in Communist Politics," in Kurt London, ed., *The Soviet Union: A Half-Century of Communism* (Baltimore: Johns Hopkins Press, 1968), p. 122; also see Frederick Barghoorn, *Politics in the USSR*, 2nd ed. (Boston: Little, Brown, 1972), esp. Chap. 8.

29. For a similar point, see Anthony Giddens, *The Class Structure of Advanced Societies*, rev. ed. (New York: Harper and Row, 1981).

30. See, for example, Albert Parry, *The New Class Divided: Science and Technology versus Communism* (New York: Macmillan, 1966); Frank Parkin, "System Contradiction and Political Transformation," *Archives Europeénes de Sociologie* 13 (1972), pp. 45–62; Ivan Szelenyi and George Konrad, *The Intellectuals on the Road to Class Power* (New York: Harcourt Brace Jovanovich, 1979); Alvin Gouldner, *The Future of the Intellectuals and the Rise of the New Class* (New York: Seabury Press, 1979).

31. See, for example, Stephen White "Contradiction and Change in State Socialism," *Soviet Studies* 26 (Jan. 1974), pp. 41–55; Marc Rakovsky, *Towards an East European Marxism* (New York: St. Martin's Press, 1978).

32. This, of course, is the official view in all socialist societies. But see also David Lane, *The Socialist Industrial State* (Boulder, Colorado: Westview Press, 1976), pp. 92–97; David Lane, "Marxist Class Conflict Analysis of State Socialist Society," in Richard Scase, ed., *Industrial Society: Class, Cleavage and Control (New York: St. Martin's Press, 1977), pp. 172–90; David Lane and Felicity O'Dell, The Soviet Industrial Worker* (New York: St. Martin's Press, 1978); and Zygmunt Bauman, "Social Dissent in the East European Political System," *Archives Europeénes de Sociologie* 12 (1971), pp. 25–51.

33. This is particularly true of Marifeli Pérez-Stable, *Politics and Conciencia*

in Revolutionary Cuba, 1959–1984 (Ph.D. diss., State University of New York at Stony Brook, 1985), which both illustrates and discusses in some detail the problems confronted by outsiders in doing survey research in Cuba.

34. Jacques Barzun and Henry F. Graff, *The Modern Researcher*, 3rd ed. (New York: Harcourt Brace Jovanovich, 1977), p. 94.

35. Eliot Friedson, "The Theory of Professions: State of the Art," in Robert Dingwall and Philip Lewis, eds., *The Sociology of the Professions* (London: Macmillan, 1983), p. 23.

36. Officially, medium-level technicians and all occupational categories above them in the Cuban system of labor categories require at least a secondary school degree. Skilled workers, on the other hand, are officially required to have only a diploma from a Polytechnical School, which requires fewer years of schooling. See UNCTAD, *Health and Education Technology in Cuba* (New York: United Nations Organization, 1979), p. 28. The education of Cuban medium-level technicians and skilled workers differs not only in extent but also in type. The Ministry of Education describes the classroom time of medium-level technicians as "30 percent practical" and of skilled workers as "60 percent practical." See Ministerio de Educación, *Cuba: organización de la educación, 1981–1983, informe a la XXXIX Conferencia Internacional de Educación, Genebra, Suiza* (Havana: 1984), p. 213.

37. For a Cuban reference to "new professionals," see the statement by the emigre accountant quoted by Roca, "State Enterprises in Cuba," p. 170.

38. For the Cuban use of "cadres," see "Sobre la política de formación, selección, ubicación, promoción y superación de los cuadros," in Primer Congreso del Partido Comunista de Cuba, *Tesis y resoluciones* (Havana: Editorial de Ciéncias Sociales, 1978), pp. 57–91.

2

Dimensions of the
Cuban Skill Problem

Representatives from all levels of Cuban society participated in the uneasy alliance of forces that struggled against the widely hated regime of Fulgencio Batista, who had forcibly taken power in 1952 through a military coup. Once the anti-Batista forces triumphed in early 1959, however, they increasingly vied with one another for control of the revolutionary movement and for the right to determine the future shape of Cuban society. As this struggle unfolded, the forces headed by Fidel Castro consolidated their control over the new regime and undertook a massive redistribution of income and wealth. Between 1959 and 1963, the Castro government halved rents, increased wages and employment, expanded health and educational services, and put 70 percent of the land and 90 to 100 percent of industry, commerce, banking, and foreign trade in the hands of the state.[1] As the regime progressed from reform to socialist revolution, wage workers and peasants rallied to its support, while the country's large property owners rapidly moved into a counterrevolutionary alliance with the United States. Situated between these two poles, Cuba's intermediate strata split into revolutionary and counterrevolutionary factions.

As a viable political alternative, the Cuban counterrevolution was relatively short-lived. The movement of a sizable portion of Cuba's intermediate strata to the counterrevolutionary pole, however, had a more enduring effect. It contributed significantly to the skill problem that would plague the revolutionary process even beyond its first decade. For, as hopes of toppling the Castro regime faded, many people from the intermediate levels left the country, taking their skills with them.

Of course, the skill problem that confronted the new revolutionary regime cannot be attributed solely to these early political struggles. This political dimension of the problem aggravated rather than caused the country's already poor skill profile. Cuba's problem of scarce, misallocated, or altogether missing skills resulted directly from the inadequate educational system of its colonial and neocolonial past. Understanding the revolution's early skill problem requires examining both its educational and political dimensions.

THE EDUCATIONAL DIMENSION

The skill problem manifested itself at all levels of Cuban society. At the lower level, it appeared most dramatically in the form of widespread illiteracy and low levels of educational achievement. According to the official census of 1953, of the 4.4 million Cubans over the age of nine, 23.6 percent were illiterate, a figure that rose to 41.7 percent in the countryside.[2] In May 1963, when over one million adult workers were tested, it was found that 55 percent demonstrated a knowledge equal to the first two grades of elementary school, 28.1 percent equal only to grades three through six, and only 5.5 percent equal to the first year of secondary school.[3]

At the levels above this, the skill problem showed up in personnel who often lacked even minimal occupational preparation. For example, the chief executive at the Banco Para el Comercio Exterior, set up by the early revolutionary government, was a twenty-seven-year-old rebel army major with only some premedical university training. His deputy had been trained as an economist, but his only experience had been in journalism. Apart from one doctor who helped with the importation of pharmaceuticals, the bank totally lacked technicians familiar with Cuba's requirements for replacement parts and raw materials. A young man with six months' experience at the National Bank was put in charge of the country's imports. A twenty-three-year-old, who had worked in an export house for a few years, was now responsible for several hundred million dollars worth of exports.[4]

This was the picture in other areas too. A Cuban study of two thousand state farms found that, in 1964, 40 percent of their administrative personnel possessed less than four years of schooling.[5] This problem persisted at least to the end of the 1960s, when the average educational level of all administrative personnel did not exceed the sixth grade. As Fidel Castro could still remark in 1970: "Signs of illiteracy and semi-literacy can be found in many men in positions of responsibility."[6]

Yet it has been said that, at the time of the revolutionary triumph, Cuba possessed the most advanced educational system in Latin America.[7] Such a comparison, however, says more about the backwardness of Latin American education in general than it does about the superiority of the Cuban system. The prerevolutionary educational system should not be judged primarily in relation to other Latin American countries; it should first be judged in terms of its quite negative role in creating the lack of relevant skills that plagued the new revolutionary regime, and its failure to keep the promise of educational opportunity that had been held out to the Cuban population and embodied in Cuban law since the beginning of the century.

The Cuban Constitution of 1901 promised no less than free compulsory schooling for all primary-school-age children, that is, for all six- to fourteen-year olds. Various laws and decrees throughout the first half of the century—in 1909, 1922, 1940, and again in 1946—reaffirmed this promise.[8] In fact, enrollment at the primary level rose to 46 percent of the relevant age cohort by 1909, and to 63 percent by 1926.[9] But this momentum was not sustained over the next three decades. The proportion of primary-school-age children attending school, according to the official census, had dropped to 55.6 percent by 1953. In the countryside, on the average only 38.7 percent of these children were enrolled, and the figure was only 26.9 percent in the poor, sugar-growing province of Oriente.[10]

With enrollment so low at the "compulsory" primary level, it is not surprising that it was even lower at the secondary level for fifteen- to nineteen-year-olds, who were not required by Cuban law to attend school. Only 16.4 percent of this age category were still in school in 1953, and the figure was just 11 percent in the poor rural province of Pinar del Rio.[11] It is also not surprising that, of college-age youths in the twenty- to twenty-four-year-old cohort, only 18 percent were still in school, and in the rural areas a mere 6.5 percent.[12]

The deficiencies of the educational system can also be seen in the population's low grade-attainment levels. According to the 1953 census, more than one and one-half million Cubans, or 31.0 percent of those over five years of age, had not even completed a first-grade education, and many of these had never attended school at all. In addition, only 56.5 percent of those over fourteen years of age had finished from five to eight grades. Only 5.6 percent of those over nineteen had completed any secondary grade. And only 2.0 percent of those over twenty-four had reached some level of university education.[13]

But even when Cuban youths had attended school and passed certain grades, their educational skill levels were still most likely quite low.

Although no achievement data exist for Cuban students in this period, there are many indications that their education lacked quality. First, although educational resources were respectable by international standards, standing at an estimated 23 percent of the state budget and at about 3 percent of national income in 1955/56,[14] maladministration and corruption ate up much of this. As one Cuban analyst pointed out, prior to the revolution a ''certain Minister of Education was known by his practice of selling classrooms, another by the use of Ministerial funds for campaigning purposes, and another by the physical appropriation of cash for himself from the Treasury vaults.''[15] Nor was corruption limited to the ministerial level. Tenured teachers at all levels were guaranteed salaries whether they worked or not. Such teachers frequently hired untrained stand-ins for themselves at much lower pay, and pocketed the difference without ever entering the classroom.[16]

Second, the methods of Cuban education had become outmoded. As a later United Nations study would point out, curricula, teaching methods, textbooks, and other course materials had been short on scientific content, and were excessively verbalistic, abstract, and formal. Rather than attempting to develop inquisitive minds and a scientific-experimental attitude, prerevolutionary Cuban education had emphasized memorizing and reciting the words of both teacher and text.[17]

Third, the content of education had been deficient and ill-suited to the country's social and economic needs. Although Cuba was, and is, primarily an agricultural country, in 1955/56 a mere 3.7 percent of its university students were studying the agricultural sciences, while some 23.0 percent were in the humanities.[18] At the secondary level, the country possessed six agricultural schools, but with a capacity of only 30 students each.[19] Consequently, in 1953 Cuba had only 294 agronomists and 355 veterinarians out of a labor force of almost two million workers.[20]

In short, the prerevolutionary educational system had taught too few students, poorly taught those it did teach, and taught them the wrong things. This inadequate system had left the most downtrodden sectors of the Cuban population hobbled by illiteracy. It had also engendered the wider problem of misallocation, scarcity, and lack of skills at all levels of Cuban society. Given this reality, it is no wonder that, as will be seen farther on, one response of the revolutionary leadership was immediately to attempt to expand and transform the educational system.

THE POLITICAL DIMENSION

One often overlooked aspect of the political dimension of the Cuban skill problem was the postrevolutionary exodus, not of Cuban nationals, but of U.S. citizens. Many of these possessed managerial and technical skills, and had occupied important posts in the U.S. corporations that had controlled much of the prerevolutionary Cuban economy. Although lack of data makes an estimate of the number of such individuals impossible, most of the higher administrative and technical personnel in U.S.-owned plants and operations had been U.S. nationals. In the U.S. oil refineries, for example, U.S. personnel commonly directed operations, while Cubans took care of maintenance and cleaning, operated cars and trucks, and served as mechanics.[21] Moreover, these highly skilled personnel left Cuba, not simply as a natural consequence of the new regime's moves to nationalize the means of production, but also as part of the early counterrevolutionary strategy of the U.S. government and corporations. The well-known oil conflict of the early years of the revolution provides a good example.[22]

In November 1959, the revolutionary government promulgated a Petroleum Law, designed to extend state control over oil exploration by U.S. petroleum companies, whose investments totaled about 147 million dollars, or about 15 percent of all direct foreign investment in the country. The law stipulated that unexploited concessions were to revert to the state and that the production royalties on oil payable to the government were to be increased from 10 percent to 60 percent. A few months later, in February 1960, the Cuban government entered into a commercial agreement with the Soviet Union to have the latter supply from 30 to 50 percent of Cuba's annual crude oil needs. This agreement benefitted the Cubans by allowing them to barter sugar for oil rather than pay in scarce hard currency, and by providing them with a better price than U.S. companies offered.

Although the U.S. companies at first appeared resigned to operating according to the new rules of the game, the U.S. government encouraged them to resist, and organized and coordinated their actions as part of a general counterrevolutionary strategy. Eventually, with State Department encouragement and help, the U.S. oil companies refused to refine Soviet crude oil, which led the revolutionary government to nationalize the industry. Along the way, however, the U.S. government-corporate alliance attempted to influence the policies of Cuba's revolutionary regime by squeezing the Cuban economy.

On May 11, 1960, for example, after the Soviet-Cuban oil agreement had been announced but before U.S. companies were requested to refine the Soviet oil, Texaco officials met with U.S. Assistant Secretary of State Rubottom to ask how the company should respond when the request to refine the Soviet oil was made. According to the State Department record of the conversation:

Table 2.1
Estimated Occupational Distribution of Cuban Refugee and Non-refugee Labor Force Participants, 1959–1962

| | A | B | C | D | E | | F | G | |
| | | | | Refugees 1959-1962 | | | | Remaining in Cuba 1962 | |
	1953	1959	Registered in U.S.	Unregistered in U.S.	In Other Countries	Total	Percentage of 1959 Total	Total	Percentage of 1959 Total
Intermediate- (and Higher-) Level Occupations									
Lawyers and Judges	7,858	9,126	1,695	925	226	2,846	31.2%	6,280	68.8%
Professional and Semiprofessional	78,051	90,646	12,124	6,615	1,617	20,356	22.5	70,290	77.5
Managers and Executives	93,662	108,776	6,771	3,694	903	11,368	10.4	97,408	89.6
Subtotal	179,571	208,548	20,590	11,234	2,746	34,570	16.6	173,978	83.4
Lower-Level Occupations									
Clerical and Sales	264,569	307,262	17,123	6,901	2,074	26,098	8.5	281,164	91.5
Domestics, Military and Police	160,406	186,291	4,801	1,935	581	7,317	3.9	178,974	96.1
Unskilled, Semi-Skilled, and Skilled	526,168	611,076	11,301	4,554	1,369	17,224	2.8	593,852	97.2
Agriculture and Fishing	807,514	937,823	1,539	620	186	2,345	0.3	935,478	99.7
Subtotal	1,758,657	2,042,452	34,764	14,010	4,210	52,984	2.6	1,989,468	97.4
Total Labor Force	1,938,228	2,251,000	55,354	25,244	6,956	87,554	3.9	2,163,446	96.1
Total Population/ Refugees	5,829,029	6,901,000	169,693	77,387	20,920	268,000	3.9%	6,633,000	96.1%

Sources: Column A: Labor force from 1953 Cuban Census as categorized by Richard Fagen, et al., Cubans in Exile: Disaffection and Revolution (Stanford: Stanford University Press, 1968), Table 2.1, p. 19; population total from Compendio anuario estadistico de la Republica de Cuba, 1976 (Cuba: Comite Estatal de Estadisticos, 1976), Table 6, p. 9.

Column B: Population total from Demographic Yearbook, Historical Supplement (New York: United Nations Organization, 1979); labor force total is the year's average as reported by Carmelo Mesa-Lago, The Labor Force, Employment, Unemployment and Underemployment in Cuba: 1899-1970 (Beverly Hills: Sage Publications, 1972), Table 12, p. 36; occupational figures estimated by the author based on assumption that each occupational category grew at same rate as labor force as a whole from 1953 to 1959.

Column C: Labor force from Fagen, Cubans in Exile, Table 2.1, p. 19, study of refugee households, registered with the Cuban Refugee Center in Miami; total registered refugees estimated by author based on assumption that proportion of labor force participants in total registered refugee population same as proportion of labor force participants in total Cuban population in 1959, i.e., 32.62 percent.

Column D: Total unregistered refugee figure equals total registered refugee figure subtracted from 247,080, the estimate of total Cuban refugees arriving in the United States between 1959 and 1962 in Juan M. Clark, The Exodus from Revolutionary Cuba (1959-1974): A Sociological Analysis (University of Florida, Ph.D. diss., 1975), Table 3, p. 74; total refugee labor force figure explained under column C, above; estimated occupational distribution figures based on widely held assumption that unregistered refugees were on the average better off than their registered counterparts and therefore more likely to come from the intermediate-level occupations. To derive these figures, I put 44.5 percent of the estimated labor force total into the intermediate-level category and 55.5 percent into the lower-level category, in accordance with Clark's estimate, pp. 214-215; I then assumed that these categories were distributed among their subtotals in the same proportions as in columns A through C.

Column E: Total refugees to non-U.S. countries from figures in columns C and D subtracted from 268,000, the estimate of total Cuban refugees to all countries between 1959 and 1962 in Clark, The Exodus, Table 3, p. 74; total labor force derived in the same fashion as the counterpart figure in column C, as explained above; occupational distribution figures based on assumption that refugees to countries other than the U.S. had occupational characteristics similar to refugees to the U.S. To derive these figures, I divided the estimated refugee labor force into 39.48 percent intermediate-level and 60.52 percent lower-level positions, the weighted average percentages for columns C and D together.

Column F: Estimated numbers the sums of columns C, D and E; estimated percentages derived by dividing column F by column B.

Column G: Estimated numbers the remainders of column B minus column F; estimated percentages derived by dividing column G by column B. To facilitate comparison with the base line year 1959, this column does not take into account labor force growth from 1959 to 1962.

Note: As parenthetically indicated on the table, some proportion of individuals in the Managers and Executives, Lawyers and Judges, and Professionals and Semi-Professionals occupational categories would appropriately be considered, not intermediate-level, but higher-level personnel. These latter would include large property owners and their close associates, the Cuban "bourgeoisie." Unfortunately, the census offers no way to separate these out. Although practically the whole Cuban bourgeoisie left in the early exodus, it was relatively small. Therefore, for the purpose at hand, it can be ignored, and these occupational categories can be considered intermediate-level, without introducing any great distortion.

25

Mr. Rubottom said that at no time had he or Mr. Dillon or other high officials
of the Department suggested that the companies should continue to ship crude
into Cuba if such action was not in accord with their own overall commercial
judgment. . . . He observed that the economic noose seems to be tightening
around Castro's neck and the country shows signs of economic strains; that it
has always been the Department's thought that the best possible solution for the
Cuban situation would be a Cuban solution. At the same time it is our thought
that at some stage we might be able and wish to contribute to this solution. This
sort of pressure which the petroleum companies can exert is one of the pressures
which the Department has always had in mind.[23]

   With this implicit State Department directive in hand, Texaco and the
other U.S. oil companies began immediately to slow their Cuban operations and to repatriate their highly skilled U.S. personnel. By the end
of May, for example, Texaco had withdrawn twenty-six of its thirty-two
U.S. employees. Although these and other withdrawn U.S. personnel did
not add up to large numbers, nevertheless because of the critical posts
such individuals occupied, they were an important element in the early
exodus of skilled personnel from the island, and contributed to the Cuban
skill problem.
   The exodus of Cuban nationals was, of course, a numerically and
politically more important aspect of the skill problem. Although Cuba's
postrevolutionary refugees have been much studied over the years, to my
knowledge no one has attempted to utilize what is known about the refugee
population and the labor force it left behind to gain a measure of the
quantitative impact of the exodus on the skill level of the remaining
Cuban population. Much is known about who left but little about who
stayed, even though it is relatively easy to estimate the relevant characteristics of the remaining population by simple subtraction.
   Practically all large property owners left the island shortly after the
revolution. They were joined by many others, but especially by incumbents of intermediate-level occupations—professionals, technicians, managers, and small business proprietors—who with their families were
overrepresented in the early years of the exodus from Cuba (see Table
2.1). Although the incumbents of intermediate-level occupations made
up less than an estimated 10 percent of the Cuban labor force in 1959,
they made up almost 40 percent of the refugees between 1959 and 1962
who had been in the Cuban labor force. Yet less than 17 percent of the
incumbents of these occupations in Cuba in 1959 actually left, while over
83 percent—the vast majority—remained in the country. Although the
rapid loss of almost 17 percent doubtless constituted a serious blow to
the country's skill profile and to the leadership's hopes for rapid economic

transformation and development, it is interesting that so many intermediate-level Cubans stayed through 1962.

Even when the makeup of the exodus is traced through 1980, the cumulative number of incumbents of intermediate-level occupations who joined the refugee flow was only 69,858 (see Table 2.2). Even if it were assumed that through these decades the Cubans merely replaced one for one the incumbents at this level remaining in Cuba but lost through retirement, death, and other non-exodus-related causes, by 1980 they would have lost through emigration only about one-third (33.5 percent) of the number of intermediate-level job holders in Cuba in 1959. Although such an assumption would, in fact, lead ultimately to a drastic underestimation of intermediate-level personnel in Cuba, in light of the dramatic expansion of Cuban secondary and higher education that the revolution eventually produced, it clearly demonstrates that, as late as 1980, Cuba had retained at least an estimated two-thirds (66.5 percent) of the number of incumbents of intermediate-level occupations that it had had in 1959. This, of course, raises the question of why, while a minority of the incumbents of this occupational stratum emigrated from the country, the vast majority stayed.

A closer look at the occupational breakdown of these intermediate-level refugees (see Table 2.1) suggests a possible answer. The fact that the occupational category most heavily affected by the exodus was that of lawyers and judges and that the least affected category was managers and executives suggests that those with skills that would be more out of tune with the new revolutionary society were much more likely to leave than those whose skills would retain more of their usefulness. For example, one would expect lawyers and judges to be tightly wedded to the old legal system and able to adapt only with great difficulty to such new forms of popular justice as the People's Courts. In other words, legal professionals would exhibit, in Thorstein Veblen's terms, a "trained incapacity" to integrate themselves into—or even to accept—the revolutionary process.

The same probability holds for much of the professional and semi-professional census category. School and university teachers made up the largest single group in this census category. Although many teachers supported the revolutionary movement, it is estimated that about 50 percent of Cuba's teachers joined the early exodus.[24] A large percentage of the refugees in the professional and semi-professional category were, therefore, teachers. One would expect many teachers, like lawyers and judges, to exhibit a trained incapacity to adapt to the revolutionary process. In fact, many teachers, by virtue of their intellectual formation in

Table 2.2
Estimated Cuban Refugee Labor Force Participants from Intermediate-Level Occupations, 1959–1980

	1959-1962	1963-1965	1966-1968	1969-1971	1972-1974	1975-1977	1978-1980	Total
Refugees	268,000	81,000	174,000	153,000	41,000	19,482	146,376	882,858
Refugee Labor Force Participants	87,554	26,422	56,785	49,909	13,374	6,355	47,748	288,147
Refugees from Intermediate- (and Higher-) Level Occupations	34,570	8,925	10,858	7,332	1,872	810	5,491	69,858
Cumulative Total of Refugees from Intermediate- (and Higher-) Level Occupations	34,570	43,495	54,353	61,685	63,557	64,367	69,858	69,858
Refugees from Intermediate-Level Occupations as a Proportion of 1959 Cuban Intermediate-Level Occupations	16.6%	20.9%	26.1%	29.6%	30.5%	30.9%	33.5%	33.5%

Sources: Refugee total for 1959-1962 from Table 2.1; for 1963-1974, from Clark, The Exodus, Table 3, p. 74; for 1975-1980, from Sergio Diaz-Briquets and Lisandro Perez, Cuba: The Demography of Revolution (Washington, D.C.: The Population Reference Bureau, 1981), Table 8, p. 26, increased by 11 percent to account for refugees to countries other than the United States, using Clark's average increment for 1959-1974.

Refugee Labor Force Participant figure for 1959-1962 from Table 2.1; for 1963-1980, 32.62 percent of the corresponding refugee figure, in accordance with rationale given under Table 2.1, column C.

Refugees from Intermediate- (and Higher-) Level Occupations for 1959-1962 from Table 2.1; for 1963-1974, computed from the percentages of "professionals" among the refugee labor force participants given by Clark, The Exodus, Figure 6, p. 74; for 1975-1977, estimated by the author at 12.75 percent, the average of Clark's figure for 1974 and the figure for 1980 in Robert L. Bach, et al., "The Flotilla 'Entrants': Latest and Most Controversial," Cuban Studies/Estudios Cubanos, 11/12 (July 1981-January 1982), Table 6, p. 43; for 1978-1980, estimated at 11.5 percent following the findings of Bach.

Refugees from Intermediate-Level Occupations as a Proportion of 1959 Intermediate-Level Occupations figures are the Cumulative Total of Refugee Intermediate-Level Occupation figures divided by the total 1959 Intermediate-Level Occupations in Table 2.1, namely 208,548.

prerevolutionary schools and their role as conveyors of conventional culture to the younger generation, seem to have been resistant to revolutionary ideology. To accept the new ideology, after all, would have brought into question much that they had taught and been taught.

Many teachers, then, seemed to perceive revolutionary change of the curriculum as an illegitimate attempt of revolutionary forces to distort the truth. As one exiled Cuban teacher explained her perception of the early revolutionary process in the schools:

We were supposed to eliminate all the materials that were not revolutionary in nature. For instance, the history books were completely eliminated. We were given guidelines about how to explain the different events in Cuban history. We were not supposed to take on our own or any explanations that had not already been confirmed by militia men that were there two or three times a week more or less instructing and telling the principal and teachers what to do and say.[25]

And as another teacher explained: "There were new books; in general most of them had political emphasis in the texts."[26] What was taught before was supposedly apolitical truth, and the new changes therefore represented for these teachers gross political distortions.

On the other hand, teachers do not just teach subject matter. They also socialize students into acceptance of the authority relations of the school, which typically reflect the social relations of the wider society. Any attempt by the revolutionary forces to alter authority in the schools would therefore be likely to be perceived by many teachers as illegitimate. Consider these two quotes from exiled Cuban teachers:

Students did not behave with the same discipline that they had before. Some of them felt very powerful, either because their families were strong supporters of the government or because they themselves had won some reputation as revolutionaries. Of course, they had a new weapon to intimidate everybody in the school, even classmates; that was to accuse them of being counterrevolutionaries.

Most [students] were our enemies and were spies. They watched the teachers all the time and the way we behaved about the revolution. In each classroom the principal had some students whose job was to watch the teachers.[27]

If it is understandable for the incumbents of occupations in law and education to show such a relatively high propensity to join the exodus, the question remains why so few in the managers and executives category left. Two reasons can be hypothesized for this. First, this category contains some small business proprietors.[28] Although many of these no doubt left Cuba in the early years in reaction to the measures of the new regime, many stayed. According to one account, moreover, these proprietors and others who joined them in the small business sector did quite well for themselves through much of the 1960s.[29] Problems with planning and the lack of strict economic controls in this period allowed the private sector to develop its relations with the state sector more or less spontaneously and to dominate the commercial trade network, especially in food. Of the enterprises engaged in commercial trade in 1967, in fact, 73.6 percent belonged to the private sector.[30] Three private concerns were reported to have each done more than five hundred thousand pesos' worth of business with state enterprises in the first half of 1967.[31] The government did not move against this small business sector until the Revolutionary Offensive of 1968, when it nationalized 58,012 private concerns.[32] Thus, many small proprietors probably stayed in Cuba because until 1968 they could do quite well.

Second, so many managers and executives probably stayed since, as the revolutionary process got under way, their economically relevant skills were in even greater demand, and their chances for moving into more responsible positions were greatly improved. As Donald Bray and Timothy Harding observed:

Although there were many working class people in high positions, most of the high government posts and the majority of the middle level bureaucracy . . . were manned by middle class individuals who had not been Communists but were nevertheless dedicated to the Revolution. . . . Most middle class administrators, technicians, guides and translators hold more responsible positions today than they would have held before the Revolution. This shift has occurred because foreigners no longer make the fundamental decisions affecting Cuba, and also, because of the emigration of skilled people and the explosion of new services and production, anyone with skill in Cuba rises rapidly to top positions.[33]

Many managers and executives thus directly benefitted from the nationalization of U.S. property, from the exodus of other skilled Cubans, and from the revolutionary transformation of the economy.

That many intermediate-level posts in revolutionary Cuba were filled by members of Cuba's prerevolutionary intermediate strata, of course, in no way proves that the majority of the intermediate actors who remained in the country was absorbed into these posts. There is no way of knowing, in fact, what proportion rose to more responsible positions, what proportion stayed at about the same level, and what proportion moved down, even to manual tasks. That many fell into the latter category, however, is indicated by the fact that revolutionary leaders have subsequently criticized the severe discrimination against the incumbents of intermediate-level occupations, and of the policy throughout the 1960s of appointing individuals to these occupations more on the basis of political than of educational credentials. Carlos Rafael Rodríguez, for one, suggested in 1972 that the revolutionary leadership did not always recognize that the intermediate strata fell into three distinct categories: (1) those with a socialist and nationalist consciousness, who were quickly integrated into the revolutionary process; (2) those with a capitalist and North American consciousness, who as rapidly as possible left the island in the first few years; and (3) those with a nonsocialist, even capitalist, consciousness, whose national consciousness nevertheless remained intact. This latter category, which Rodríguez suggested could have been integrated into the revolution, was in fact discriminated against.[34]

Although many in this latter category joined the exodus, others endured unhappy discrimination in Cuba. In 1980, I interviewed a man who before the revolution was a college-educated technician for one of the U.S. oil companies in Cuba.[35] In the 1960s, he was prevented from pursuing this or any other technical occupation, and was forced into various types of manual labor, usually in the sugar sector. Other than his protestation that he never opposed the revolution, there is no way of knowing the character of his political consciousness or activities in the early years of the revolution. But when I spoke with him he expressed great pride in the revolution's accomplishments. He was also proud that he was again a technician in the now-Cuban oil industry, and that his three children were either new professionals or new professionals-in-training. His oldest child was a professor and his two younger ones were both university students. Obviously, in his own terms, this individual's endurance had paid off. Other stories doubtlessly ended less happily.

It is clear, then, that, while the intermediate occupational strata were overrepresented in the early years of the exodus from revolutionary Cuba, a clear majority of individuals at this level remained in the country. The analysis here suggests that at least one important factor influencing who within these occupations would leave and who would stay was the character of their skills and their ability to use them within the new revolutionary society. Those whose skills resulted in a trained incapacity to adapt to the revolutionary process, or whose skills were made irrelevant by the changing legal, political, and economic structures, or by official discrimination, were probably more likely to emigrate. Those whose skills could easily be put to use in the new revolutionary society were undoubtedly more likely to stay.

In sum, the skill problem faced by the early revolutionary regime had both educational and political dimensions. On the one hand, this problem arose directly from the inadequacies of the prerevolutionary Cuban educational system. On the other, it was aggravated considerably by the early revolutionary political struggles, which pulled apart Cuba's intermediate strata into revolutionary and counterrevolutionary factions. In the course of these struggles, many U.S. and Cuban nationals, who had previously performed intermediate-level occupational roles, took their skills with them out of the country. And, although at least two-thirds of the intermediate-level individuals remained on the island, the changed legal, political, and economic systems, or official discrimination, prevented some from plying their skills. Whatever the exact contribution of each of these factors to the skill problem, the problem was severe, and it called forth a variety of official responses throughout the 1960s.

NOTES

1. José Acosta, "Cuba: de la neocolonia a la construcción del socialismo (II)," *Economía y Desarrollo* 19 (Nov.-Dec. 1973), p. 79.

2. Oficina Nacional de los Censos Demográfica y Electora, *Censos de población, viviendos y electoral* (Havana: 1953), p. xxxix.

3. UNCTAD, *Health and Education Technology in Cuba* (New York: United Nations Organization, 1979), p. 11.

4. Edward Boorstein, *The Economic Transformation of Cuba* (New York: Monthly Review Press, 1968), pp. 63–64.

5. Cited in Nelson P. Valdés, *Cuba: socialismo democrático o bureaucratismo colectivista* (Bogotá: Ediciones Tercer Mundo, 1973), p. 19.

6. Fidel Castro, "Report on the Cuban Economy" in Rolando Bonachea and Nelson Valdés, eds., *Cuba in Revolution* (Garden City, New York: Doubleday, 1972), p. 338.

7. CEPAL, *Cuba: estilo de desarrollo y políticos sociales* (Cerro del Agua, México: Siglo Veintiuno Editores, 1980), p. 87.

8. Richard Jolly, "Education" in Dudley Seers, ed., *Cuba: The Economic and Social Revolution* (Chapel Hill: University of North Carolina Press, 1964), p. 25.

9. UNCTAD, p. 3.

10. *Censos de población*, p. xxxviii.

11. Ibid., p. xxxix.

12. Author's computations based on ibid., p. 99.

13. Author's computations based on ibid., p. 119.

14. UNCTAD, p. 4.

15. Jorge García Gallo, "Bosquejo general del desarrollo de la educación en Cuba (Tercera Parte)," *Educación*, July-Sept. 1974, p. 32.

16. UNCTAD, p. 4.

17. Ibid.

18. Ibid., p. 32.

19. Ibid., p. 27.

20. *Censos de población*, p. 204.

21. Boorstein, *Economic Transformation of Cuba*, p. 55.

22. The following account of the oil conflict is taken from the excellent discussion of Morris Morley, *Toward a Theory of Imperial Politics: United States Policy and the Processes of State Formation, Disintegration and Consolidation in Cuba, 1898–1978* (Ph.D. diss., State University of New York at Binghamton, 1980), pp. 428–38.

23. Memorandum of Conversation, U.S. Department of State, May 11, 1960, Subject: "Difficulties of the Texas Company in Cuba with regard to dollar remittances and concern at possibility it will be asked to refine Russian crude oil," 837.131/5–1160 (declassified Freedom of Information Act), cited in ibid., p. 430.

24. Author's interview HG01.80, with a Cuban government official.

25. Eugene F. Provenzano and Concepción García, "Exiled Teachers and the Cuban Revolution," *Cuban Studies/Estudios Cubanos*, 13, 1 (Winter 1983), p. 2.

26. Ibid., p. 7.

27. Ibid., p. 9.

28. See *Censos de población*, p. 204. Unfortunately, the census data are not sufficiently disaggregated to allow an estimate of the proportion of small business proprietors.

29. Hector Ayala Castro, "Transformación de propiedad en el período 1964–1980," *Economía y Desarrollo*, 68 (May-June 1982), pp. 11–25.

30. Ibid., p. 18.

31. Ibid.

32. Ibid., p. 19.

33. Donald W. Bray and Timothy F. Harding, "Cuba," in Ronald H. Chilcote and Joel C. Edelstein, eds., *Latin America: The Struggle with Dependency and Beyond* (Cambridge, Massachusetts: Schenkman Publishing, 1974), pp. 620–21.

34. Carlos Rafael Rodríguez, "En el proceso de construcción del socialismo la política debe tener prioridad," *Economía y Desarrollo* 14 (Nov.-Dec. 1972), pp. 144–57.

35. Author's interview HNGT4.80.

3

Responses to the Skill Problem in Revolutionary Cuba, and the Crisis of 1970

As the Cuban revolutionary leadership took the bulk of productive property into state hands and consolidated its political base through income redistribution, it also attended to economic development. In its first development strategy (1961–1963), the regime strove to move away from sugar monoculture through immediate agricultural diversification and industrialization.[1] But balance of trade and other economic difficulties soon emerged. Because this first strategy was severely impeded by the U.S. blockade and embargo, and because it proved poorly suited to Cuba's natural resources and human skills at the time, it became clear that a new strategy would have to be pursued.

In its second development strategy (1964–1970), the regime reverted to agricultural specialization and undertook a "big push" to produce a record ten million tons of sugar in 1970.[2] In 1964, the Soviet Union guaranteed the reliable and expanding market required by this strategy: They agreed to increase their imports of Cuban sugar to five million tons annually from 1968 through 1970 and to pay the then high price of 6.11 cents per pound. The Cubans would sell the other five tons of sugar on the world market for hard currency. Export of this ten million tons of sugar would allow Cuba to begin equalizing its balance of payments and start importing sufficient capital goods for a new, more secure round of industrialization. Emphasizing sugar and other agricultural products, this strategy was based on Cuba's soil and climate conditions and on its large sugar-processing industry and accumulated know-how and skills.[3]

As the regime pursued economic development, it attacked the skill problem from two sides. On the supply side, even before it instituted the first development strategy, the revolutionary leadership was working to increase the supply of skills by expanding and transforming the educational system. Although impressive, its educational successes over the decade were less than expected. By 1970, it became clear that the "big push" to produce ten million tons of sugar had begun to erode some earlier educational gains. On the demand side, especially during the second development strategy, the revolutionary leadership introduced organizational structures and motivational mechanisms designed to minimize the demand for relatively skilled intermediate-level personnel. Although most economists have criticized this second strategy, especially the 10-million-ton goal for sugar, as overly ambitious, at least one analyst has appraised it more positively.[4] Whatever the case from a strictly economic viewpoint, the mix of the second strategy with the organizational structures and motivational mechanisms to implement it, which were designed in part to deal with the skill problem, proved volatile: This mix exploded in the political and economic crisis of 1970.

INCREASING THE SUPPLY OF SKILLS

Educational expansion began almost immediately with the revolutionary triumph. The most dramatic push, however, came in 1961, the "Year of Education," with its well-known literacy campaign. This campaign was officially opened on January 1, 1961. The slogans "The People Should Teach the People" and "If You Do Not Know, Learn; If You Know, Teach!" were spread throughout the island until the campaign officially ended on December 22, 1961.[5] In all, an estimated 271,000 Cubans participated as voluntary teachers in this campaign.[6] In only one year, these reduced Cuba's illiteracy rate from 23.6 to 3.9 percent.[7]

Although the literacy campaign was an astounding success, it was only a beginning. In order for the literacy skills gained during the campaign not to be lost, they had to be built upon and reinforced. Within a month of the end of the campaign, the revolutionary leadership addressed this need by forming a department of adult education within the Ministry of Education. Out of this eventually grew a full-scale adult education system parallel to the regular system at the primary and secondary levels.[8]

Enrollment in adult education rose dramatically from 66,577 students in the 1960/61 school year to a peak of 842,024 students in 1964/65, but then plummeted to 306,917 students by 1969/70 (see Table 3.1). Because of this drop, the "Battle for the Sixth Grade," which had been launched

Table 3.1

Adult, Primary, Secondary, and Higher Education Enrollments in Cuba, 1958/59 to 1969/70

School Year	Enrollment			
	Adult	Primary	Secondary	Higher [a]
1958/59	N.A.	625,729	88,135	N.A.
1959/60	N.A.	950,217	90,660	25,295
1960/61	66,577	1,029,923	122,897	19,454
1961/62	439,042	1,088,016	151,826	17,888
1962/63	499,925	1,137,479	182,981	17,257
1963/64	476,328	1,225,539	216,849	20,393
1964/65	842,024	1,246,381	217,014	26,271
1965/66	574,683	1,242,256	231,317	26,162
1966/67	451,499	1,266,240	255,127	28,243
1967/68	499,980	1,279,695	288,748	29,238
1968/69	373,211	1,341,728	276,303	32,327
1969/70	306,917	1,427,607	276,209	34,520

Source: Ministerio de Educación, Informe a la Asamblea Nacional del Poder Popular (Havana: 1981), pp. 344-347.

a. Includes all university-level day, evening, and correspondence courses.

in 1964 to bring the adult population up to the sixth grade level, had not been won by the end of the 1960s.[9] Also perhaps partly as a result of this drop, the illiteracy rate reportedly had risen to 12.9 percent by 1970.[10]

The dramatic drop in adult education enrollments in the second half of the 1960s was a direct result of the second economic development strategy. Not only did the push to produce ten million tons of sugar divert and devour resources that could have been used to educate adults, it also drew many adults away from classroom study and into the sugar fields as voluntary laborers. Moreover, as will be seen farther on, in the period of the second strategy the trade unions and other mass organizations, which were largely responsible for furthering adult education, were seriously weakened.

Unlike adult education, primary-level schooling continued to expand throughout the first decade of the revolution. In the 1958/59 school year, 625,729 students were enrolled at the primary level; by 1969/70 this figure had jumped to 1,427,607 (see Table 3.1). This steady increase, however, hid a complex of underlying problems. Part of this increase was made necessary by the fact that many students, who had either dropped out of school during the year or failed, had to repeat their grade. Of the class that entered first grade in 1964 and was scheduled to complete sixth grade in 1970, only 20.7 percent were graduated on time.[11] In other words, much of the expansion of primary education was made necessary by the inefficiency of the system itself.

Secondary education in Cuba also expanded dramatically with the revolution. However, by 1970/71 only 63.8 percent of thirteen- to sixteen-year-old Cubans were in school. Although this was a vast improvement over the 1953 figure of 39.8 percent, by the end of the 1960s Cuban secondary education still required further expansion.[12] Moreover, as in adult education, secondary education enrollments began to contract in the late 1960s (see Table 3.1). Enrollments at this level steadily increased from 88,135 students in 1958/59 to 288,748 students by 1967/68, and then dipped to 276,209 students by 1969/70. This decline can be attributed to several factors. On the one hand, stagnation in the number of primary school students who actually graduated from sixth grade meant fewer students available for secondary education. On the other hand, as with adult students, many students in secondary education were probably pulled out of the classroom and into the sugar fields during the second development strategy.

Although considerably transformed, higher education was the least expansive sector through the 1960s. At the time of the revolutionary triumph, Cuba possessed only three public universities, at Havana, Las Villas, and Santiago, one private university, and several private colleges. During the revolutionary struggle, Batista had closed the public institutions because of the opposition they spawned, but he allowed the private institutions, with their more supportive or at least more silent faculty and students, to remain open. Soon after the triumph, the revolutionary leadership reopened the public universities, and in 1961 it abolished the private ones. In 1962, the new leadership consolidated all institutions of higher education under the Ministry of Education, and promulgated a far-reaching reform of the whole higher education system.[13] But expansion of higher education did not immediately follow.[14]

Higher education enrollments actually dropped in the early years of the revolution, to reach a low of 17,257 in 1962/63, and they did not recover their 1959/60 level until 1964/65 (see Table 3.1). One reason for this drop was the relative unavailability of qualified secondary school graduates in this period. A second perhaps more significant reason was the intense ideological struggle that took place in the universities over the extension of higher education to workers and peasants and over the character and content of the education that should be provided. Although

Table 3.2

Primary, Secondary, and Higher Education Enrollments as a Percentage of Total Enrollments in Cuba, 1959/60 and 1970/71

| School Year | Enrollment | | | |
	Primary	Secondary	Higher	Total
1959/60	89.1%	8.5%	2.4%	100.0%
1970/71	83.3	14.8	1.9	100.0

Source: Author's computations based on Minsterio de Educación, Informe a la Asamblea Nacional del Poder Popular (Havana: 1981), pp. 344-346.

the majority of the student body supported the new government's push to revolutionize higher education, many faculty and some students did not. These opponents often left the university to join counterrevolutionary organizations or to join the exodus out of Cuba.[15]

After this initial drop, higher education enrollments began a steady, if relatively gradual, climb to 34,520 in 1969/70. However, much of this expansion was wasted. In 1968/69, for example, a full 50 percent of first-year enrollees at the university level failed to pass in the initial year. Systematic study of the predominant causes of failure was not even undertaken until 1969/70. And corrective measures were not taken until 1971/72.[16]

The pattern of higher education enrollments can be illustrated in another manner. As the educational level of the population rose over the 1960s, enrollments at the primary level decreased as a percentage of total enrollments, while enrollments at the secondary level increased (see Table 3.2). This increase, however, did not extend to the higher education level. As a percentage of total enrollments, higher education enrollments, in fact, dropped from 2.4 percent in 1959/60 to 1.9 percent in 1970/71.

Besides these causes for the drop in enrollments during the early 1960s, two other reasons can explain the relatively slow growth and relative decline of higher education enrollments as a percentage of total enrollments in the 1960s. First and most obvious is the fact that, before higher education could be expanded dramatically, both primary and secondary education had to expand and become more efficient. And it was on the latter two levels that the revolutionary government concentrated in the 1960s. Second, due to the scarcity of skilled personnel in the 1960s, many would-be candidates for university training were pulled into the labor force rather than into schools. One can still find in Cuba skilled personnel in intermediate occupations whose education was interrupted by the needs of economic development and who are just now gaining undergraduate and graduate degrees.[17]

In the 1960s, higher education in Cuba was not simply expanded, it was transformed in character and content as well. The 1962 reform of higher education eliminated tenure for faculty members, set faculty salaries, restructured the university governance system, set entrance requirements for students, and much else. But perhaps the most significant change was the restructuring of course and subject areas and the redistribution of enrollment by subject area. As the reform document emphasized, a major problem with Cuban education had been the lack of fit between the knowledge imparted and the needs of economic development.[18] This, the reform sought to change.

Enrollment in higher education subject areas changed considerably in the 1960s (see Table 3.3). On the one hand, subject areas directly related to economic development or social service needs expanded the most rapidly. Between 1959/60 and 1969/70, agricultural sciences enrollments went from 759 to 5,154, an increase of almost 580 percent. That this subject area expanded more than any other reflected the agricultural emphasis of the second economic development strategy and the ten-million-ton sugar goal. In this same period, the subject areas of technology, natural and exact sciences, and medical sciences had substantial but more moderate enrollment increases. On the other hand, the 42 percent drop in humanities, social sciences, and art enrollments illustrates the deemphasis of subject areas not directly related to economic development in the 1960s.

Less obviously consistent with this pattern, however, are the enrollment drops in education and economic studies. Education enrollments dropped in the 1960s from 5,180 to 1,627, or by 68.6 percent. This might at first be surprising, because, as has already been seen, both primary and secondary enrollments, and therefore the need for teachers, increased in these years. Some of this drop in education enrollments can probably be explained by an excessive enthusiasm for the use of "amateur" teachers that resulted from the remarkable results obtained in the literacy campaign.[19] In fact, scarcity of resources made it imperative for the Cubans to rely for many years on less-trained teachers who were often only a few grades ahead of their pupils. But this could hardly justify an actual drop in education enrollments. As the Cubans eventually recognized, this drop aggravated many of the problems in the educational system touched on above.[20] But this drop would not be reversed until after 1970.

Table 3.3

Cuban Higher Education Enrollments by Subject Area, 1959/60 and 1969/70

Subject Area	Enrollment 1959/60	1969/70	Percentage Change 1959/60 - 1969/70
Agricultural Sciences	759	5,154	579.1%
Technology	3,211	7,948	147.5
Natural and Exact Sciences	1,479	3,420	131.2
Medical Sciences	3,947	7,977	102.1
Humanities, Social Sciences, and Art	3,757	2,178	-42.0
Education	5,180	1,627	-68.6
Economic Studies	5,144	1,214	-76.4
Total	23,478	29,518	25.7

Source: Ministerio de Educación Superior, Informe de la delegación de la Republica de Cuba a la VII Conferencia de Ministros de Educación Superior y Media Especializada de los Países Socialistas (Havana: 1972), pp. 117-118. All percentage change figures computed by author.

Note: The total enrollment figures from this source are somewhat lower than those in Table 3.1. The most likely reason for this discrepancy is that this source may not include some categories of higher education enrollments, such as in correspondence courses. This source is used here because it gives a breakdown of enrollment by "Faculty," labeled "Subject Area" on this table.

The 76.4 percent drop of enrollments in economic studies[21] between 1959/60 and 1969/70 is especially interesting, because it reflects the major policy shifts of the revolutionary leadership over the 1960s. This drop was probably not linear. In the early 1960s, before and during the first economic development strategy, the leadership in fact greatly emphasized the need for increased numbers of economic professionals. As early as March 2, 1960, then Minister of Industry Ernesto "Che" Guevara, in a speech at the University of Havana, called for establishing a school to train Cuban economic professionals to replace the many foreign ones on whom the revolution was dependent for teaching, and for planning and administering its increasingly collectivized economy. Due to the intense political struggle that took place at the University of Havana in this period, however, no such school was established until 1962 with the reform of higher education.

Even then, however, the need for trained economic planners, evaluators, and analysts was too great to wait the five years necessary to produce the first cohort of graduates. As a result, in the same year an emergency Course for Planners was implemented to train economic professionals in one and one-half and later two years. By 1964, this emergency course was eliminated, perhaps because it was not doing the job, and its students were placed in regular courses at the University of Havana. In this same period, various ministries set up their own crash courses to train their own economic personnel as quickly as possible.

One critical problem faced in these initial attempts to train economic professionals was Cuba's lack of a strong tradition of economic studies, which, coupled with the early exodus of a majority of the members of the Faculty of Commercial Sciences at the University of Havana, resulted in a severe shortage of teachers. To address this problem, about forty revolutionary students were chosen for intense preparation by Latin American and Soviet professors to become the nucleus of a future economic studies faculty. In 1965, economic studies at the University of Havana were upgraded through separation from the Faculty of Humanities, and a separate Institute of Economy (Instituto de Economía) was established.

This extensive initial effort in higher economic studies education suggests that enrollments probably increased in the first half of the 1960s, and dropped only in the second half. This would also be consistent with the fact that in the late 1960s, the Cuban leadership, like such Marxists of an earlier generation as Nikolai Bukharin and Rosa Luxemburg, came to view economics as a science of bourgeois society that had lost its relevance with the advent of socialism.[22] As a result, in 1967 courses in the political economy of socialism were abolished. The discipline of accounting was looked down upon, and its name was changed to "economic control," to eliminate any commercial connotation. Many textbooks were jettisoned, often replaced by the political pronouncements of revolutionary leaders.

In 1970, Osvaldo Dorticós described the prevailing leadership attitude in the late 1960s. Although it had always been recognized, he stated, that to be an engineer, architect, or medical doctor required formal training, it had recently been widely believed that economic and administrative posts required nothing more than revolutionary consciousness and personal experience on the job.[23] As will be seen in the next section, this attitude was intimately connected with the second economic development strategy, especially the organizational structures and motivational mechanisms used in the late 1960s to implement it. Of course, such an attitude easily led to a downgrading of economic studies and a drop in enrollments in this area.

To summarize, in the 1960s the revolutionary leadership responded to the supply side of the skill problem by dramatically expanding and transforming the educational system at all levels. But, although educational progress was impressive in this period, a variety of problems remained; by the end of the decade, many earlier advances were being lost. As will be seen in Chapter 5, by the beginning of the 1970s progress in secondary and higher education had been only sufficient to just barely compensate for the drain of skills through the exodus of intermediate-level personnel from the country. By the end of the 1960s the skill problem, although mitigated to some extent, remained severe. As a result, throughout the 1960s the revolutionary leadership searched for organizational and motivational models that would minimize the need for many, especially intermediate-level administrative, skills.

MINIMIZING THE DEMAND FOR SKILLS

Organizational structures and motivational mechanisms were first seriously discussed in the so-called Great Debate that raged in Cuba between 1962 and 1965.[24] This debate had many facets and ranged over such issues as Marxist theory on the socialist transition, the nature of socialist and communist morality, and even the nature of the human species. In immediate practical terms, the antagonists argued for the exclusive use of one of two organizational and motivational models.

One of these approaches was used at the time in the agricultural sector, and was then called the "auto-finance" system. This system decentralized many economic decisions down to the enterprises, which served as semi-autonomous centers of production, resource allocation, accounting, and profit realization. The activities of these enterprises were coordinated through a combination of central planning and market mechanisms, and their workers were motivated primarily by personal and material incentives.

The other mechanism then operated in the industrial sector, and was called the "centralized budgetary" system. This system sought to centralize economic decisions, and to relieve enterprises of autonomy. The activities of enterprises were coordinated, not at all by market mechanisms, but totally by central planning and budgetary controls. Workers in this system were to be motivated by personal material incentives to fulfill production quotas, but only moral incentives would be offered for overfulfillment. Although personal material incentives would be offered, collective and moral incentives would predominate and as quickly as possible replace personal material gain altogether.

As Che Guevara, the leading proponent of the centralized budgetary model, made clear, each side in the Great Debate argued that, compared to the other, its own model would minimize the demand for skills by requiring a smaller administrative apparatus and fewer trained personnel to operate it. Guevara countered the proponents of the auto-finance system who claimed that his centralized budgetary model had

a tendency toward bureaucracy. One point must therefore be constantly stressed: The entire administrative apparatus must be organized on a rational basis. Now, from the standpoint of objective analysis, it is obvious that there will be less bureaucracy the more centralized are enterprises or production units, recording and controlling operations. If every enterprise could centralize all its administrative activities, its bureaucracy would be reduced to a small nucleus of unit directors plus someone to collect information for headquarters.[25]

Guevara was well aware that, to the extent it was implemented in the industrial sector, his model never operated in this lean, well-organized fashion. He complained in 1963, for example, that "a goodly number of civil servants put in requests for more personnel as their only means of carrying out a task otherwise quite easily solved by a little brain power."[26] This tendency to bloat the administrative apparatus doubtless stemmed in part from the fact that many members of the apparatus, although professional revolutionaries, were appointed for political more than educational credentials, and were still amateur administrators. But Guevara still maintained that his model best compensated for the skill problem, so long as the administrative apparatus was strictly organized.

During the Great Debate, Fidel Castro had never taken a public position on which of the organizational and motivational models should be preferred. But, as the debate subsided in 1965 and all major theoretical journals were shut down—the order of the day was to produce, not debate—what has been called a *fidelista* model was imposed on the economy.[27] Along with unique features of its own, this eclectically combined elements from both the auto-finance and centralized budgetary models.

With Guevara and other proponents of the centralized budgetary model, the adherents of the *fidelista* model shared an emphasis on the importance of using moral incentives to create a "New Person" who would unselfishly sacrifice for the common good.[28] Whatever broader philosophical notions underlay this view, both Guevara and supporters of the *fidelista* model considered the need for a New Person to be based in the material reality of revolutionary Cuba. First, they claimed that Cuba was simply too poor to rely primarily on personal material incentives. As Fidel Castro would later explain: "our poor countries . . . have very little to give on the material level. If they want to give goods they can't, and if they convert material goods into the main motivation they fail."[29]

Second, having radically redistributed wealth and income and introduced a host of egalitarian measures that seriously weakened the incentive structure of capitalism, with its promise of personal material gain and threat of unemployment, Guevara and the adherents of the *fidelista* model felt compelled to find collective and moral motivations for work. Third, to permit the high rates of capital formation and the labor-intensive development projects considered necessary to develop the material base of the future society, they needed a New Person who would work long and hard, not for personal advantage, but for the good of the community. Although everyone would benefit from enormously expanded opportunities for collective consumption (e.g., free health and educational services), for the sake of economic development, the New Person's wants and personal consumption would have to remain austere. Guevara and the proponents of the *fidelista* model, in short, considered the New Person the precondition for economic advance in revolutionary Cuba.

When the supporters of the *fidelista* model were not simply assuming that the New Person already universally existed in Cuba, they utilized a host of mechanisms, from egalitarian distribution and moral rewards to voluntary labor and ideological exhortation to create such a person. But, unlike Guevara, they never seem to have given much thought to the organizational prerequisites for the development of the New Person. Rightly or wrongly, Guevara argued that only his highly centralized and rationalized model could accomplish the task. Not only would his model eliminate capitalist market relations among production units and move rapidly toward eliminating personal material incentives for individual workers, but it would construct a unified economic organization to make all individuals feel part of a single social whole to which they could relate with a profound collective consciousness. A truly collective and rationally organized economic structure was needed to form the objective basis for the subjective collective sense.[30] At least in intention, Guevara approached the creation of a New Person practically, objectively. The adherents of the *fidelista* model, as will be illustrated below, approached the question idealistically, or subjectively.

On the other hand, like the auto-finance model, the *fidelista* model allowed enterprises to operate semi-autonomously, but not only without effective central but also without market coordination. In late 1965, for example, revolutionary leaders abolished the Ministry of Finance and reduced the power of the National Bank. In 1966, they weakened the Central Planning Agency (Junta Central de Planificación—JUCEPLAN), which had directed all macro-economic plans; and they adopted regional and local mini-plans, without coherently connecting them. They provided for the decentralized allocation of resources, but without using market mechanisms. In 1967, they abolished all payments and receipts by state enterprises, all taxes, and all interest on bank credits. By 1968, they had stopped preparing a national budget for the entire economy.

According to some scholars, the imposition of the *fidelista* model in the late 1960s was a movement toward greater decentralization;[31] according to others, it was a movement toward greater centralization.[32] Both are accurate, but each only with respect to particular aspects of the system. Certainly the power to make decisions affecting the whole society, the most dramatic example being the ten-million-ton sugar goal for 1970, remained concentrated in the hands of the revolutionary leadership, as did the designing of the mini-plans. Only the implementation of such decisions were decentralized. As controls over production units were lessened, many administrative personnel were sent to the fields and factories to solve production problems on the ground. The basic operations, with few administrative overseers to check their work, were implemented with a great deal of autonomy.

This led to many different local solutions or near solutions and, from a societal point of view, much chaos. When decisions were not satisfactorily implemented, however, especially when this involved an economic area considered critical, the revolutionary leadership often intervened directly to impose its own plan for implementation at the base. Intervention often took place through the Party or the Revolutionary Armed Forces, which led some commentators to speak of growing centralization of power and militarization in this period. Thus, depending on which aspect of this movement one cares to emphasize, it can be viewed as a movement either toward decentralization or toward centralization. In fact, it was an historically specific combination of both.

Instead of strictly organizing the administrative apparatus in accordance with either the auto-finance or the centralized budgetary models, the backers of the *fidelista* model radically shook it up and attempted to reduce its size. In a central document, which appeared as a series of editorials in *Granma* during May 1967, revolutionary leaders declared an "anti-bureaucratic revolution."[33] They attempted to pare the administrative apparatus to a minimum. They frequently rotated administrative personnel to prevent the "tendency to settle in and consider oneself 'indispensable.' "[34] They sent administrative personnel out of their offices to deal with production problems on the spot rather than sit behind their desks and shuffle papers. Fewer administrative personnel, fewer rules to be imposed on production units, less information and fewer forms to be sent up and down the administrative apparatus, less red tape altogether, these were the goals of the anti-bureaucratic revolution. With fewer administrative controls over lower levels, fewer administrative controllers were needed, and administrative personnel were often required to engage in "productive," that is, manual labor. In the *fidelista* period, Fidel Castro, decked out in worker's mufti, himself posed for an occasional snapshot swinging a machete among the sugar stalks.[35]

In response to the scarcity of administrative skills, then, the supporters of the *fidelista* model, like the proponents of both the auto-finance and the centralized budgetary models, but much more radically, pushed for a lean organizational structure. The backers of the *fidelista* model, however, did not attempt to compensate for scarce skills through rational organization. Rather, at least temporarily, while the overriding goal was the production of ten million tons of sugar, they tended to deny the usefulness of such skills. They failed to use even the skills available, and involved many administrative personnel directly in production. They failed, as seen in the last section, to create many new skills that they could have used. And, most important for future developments, they pushed to an extreme the practice of appointing administrative personnel on the basis of political rather than educational credentials.[36] As will be seen in Chapter 5, despite their few skills and often inefficient work styles, these personnel would retain administrative posts for a long time to come.

Proponents of the *fidelista* model denied the usefulness of such skills for two reasons. First, this denial represented an explosion of a long-accumulated and widespread Cuban perception of the prerevolutionary intermediate strata as politically unreliable, rampantly corrupt, and economically parasitical. Such a perspective, shared by the revolutionary leadership and workers alike, had already resulted in discrimination

against many individuals, and it was now projected onto many intermediate-level occupations, regardless of the social origins of their incumbents. In this sense, the *fidelista* doctrine marked the zenith of
discrimination against prerevolutionary intermediate strata.[37]

Second, the adherents of the *fidelista* model denied the usefulness of
many administrative skills because of the pressures of their own ten-
million-ton sugar goal. As problems emerged in realizing this goal, the
revolutionary leadership pushed all the harder in attempting to mobilize
all available labor to meet the goal. They apparently concluded that what
was needed was not skills but individuals willing to callous their hands.
The political consciousness of the New Person would compensate for
scarce skills.

THE CRISIS OF 1970

A few key economic indicators illustrate the overall results of the
fidelista implementation of the second development strategy. Although
this strategy envisioned a 14 percent annual growth rate through 1970,
in 1975 Fidel Castro stated that the actual rate had been only 4 percent,
and outside commentators have typically put it even lower.[38] Moreover,
although a record 8.5 million tons of sugar were produced in 1970, this
fell short of the ten-million-ton goal and continued the pattern of sugar
shortfalls that had begun in 1966. Sugar production was never less than
15 percent below plan between 1966 and 1970, and in 1969 it fell a full
50 percent below plan.[39]

Even with this, the effort to reach the 10-million-ton goal diverted
resources to the sugar sector and starved many nonsugar operations. In
1970, steel deliveries were 38 percent below plan, soap production 32
percent, and butter production 33 percent. In addition, production of
liquid milk, vegetables, root crops, beans, meat, and poultry in 1970 all
fell below 1969 levels. In 1970, the record gains in sugar production
were probably outpaced by losses in the rest of the economy.[40]

The *fidelista* model, with its weakened central controls and mini-plans,
led to the waste of many resources, which had not only economic but
also political implications. It helped undercut the New Person strategy
of developing collective consciousness. As the revolutionary leadership
pushed the investment rate to new heights, personal consumption, although equalized through rationing and cushioned by expanded collective
consumption, was generally depressed.[41] Encouraged to work long and
hard while suffering low levels of personal consumption, even the most
committed New Person could become disillusioned when effort and sac-

rifice did not result in promised economic results. By wasting material and human resources, the revolutionary leadership was wasting the people's labor. Willingness to sacrifice, revolutionary enthusiasm, collective consciousness—the coinage of the *fidelista* model—were being poorly spent.

The operation of the *fidelista* system of labor mobilization and incentives makes this very clear. In the late 1960s, massive numbers of individuals were mobilized for voluntary labor, especially in agriculture, participation in which was to instill New Person attitudes. Such voluntary labor took several forms. Sometimes workers would volunteer to work without pay after their regular jobs, on weekends, or on holidays. Sometimes whole production units would commit themselves to voluntary labor. Some of their number would go off to the sugar fields, for example, while being paid their regular wages, and their remaining coworkers would compensate for their absence with more intensive labor or unpaid overtime. Sometimes housewives or others not in the regular labor force would volunteer for unpaid work.

Regardless of its form, much voluntary labor was irrationally used. In the *fidelista* period, its success was typically judged by the number of hours worked, whatever its output. Stories abound of volunteers transported to projects that were ill-conceived, poorly organized, or lacking in necessary tools and materials. Productivity on many projects was extremely low, and many projects cost more in transport and fuel than they created in output. As a result, many projects produced only lower morale for their participants.[42]

The *fidelista* incentive system, as seen above, emphasized moral over material incentives. Work norms, for example, which had been instituted in 1961, fell into disuse after 1966. Between 1961 and 1966 wages had been cut by the amount that output quotas were unmet, and bonuses were paid at the rate of 50 percent of the amount by which quotas were exceeded. But after 1966 workers were seldom materially penalized for not reaching quotas, and it became a sign of revolutionary commitment to forego bonuses. According to then Minister of Labor Jorge Risquet:

Even though legally in force, fines, suspensions, etc., are typically capitalist sanctions . . . and we have refrained from imposing them. . . . Sanctions must be the last resort. Education and re-education through collective self-criticism and the help of other workers are the basic weapons in this struggle.[43]

Thus to develop the New Person, "capitalist sanctions," that is, material incentives, were replaced with moral ones.

This is not to say, however, that material incentives disappeared altogether. Regular work was still remunerated through wages, with different wage levels for different types of work. Like all socialist incentive systems, the *fidelista* system was mixed. Official wage scales were only slightly differentiated and such inequalities as did occur from wage differences were mitigated by free services and rationing at set prices. Nevertheless, significant inequalities arose from the actual wage. The policy of the revolutionary leadership was to equalize wages from the bottom up, not from the top down, as productivity increases made this possible.[44] This meant that so-called historical wages, that is, wage levels carried over from the prerevolutionary past, would be eliminated very slowly, and mostly through attrition. During his 1967 visit to the Nicaro Nickel Plant, K. S. Karol found engineers earning historical wages up to 1,700 pesos per month, while new engineers working under official wage scales were earning from 300 to 400 pesos per month, and average production workers made only 100 pesos per month.[45]

Such widely divergent pay for similar work, however, did not just result from historical wages. Other out-of-line wages, as they were called, derived not from the capitalist past but from the administrative inefficiencies of the revolutionary present. Because of incorrect evaluation, work requiring fewer skills or less effort was often relatively over-remunerated in comparison to work requiring more skills or more effort. Also, as production units were merged or otherwise rationalized, and particular jobs eliminated or transformed, workers whose jobs became less demanding were often paid at their old higher wage, while new workers received remuneration in accord with the lower official scales. Even workers who voluntarily transferred to less demanding jobs continued to receive their old wages. How widespread such inequities were is hard to judge, but, according to one Cuban official, they still affected "a significant percentage . . . of Cuban workers as late as 1975."[46]

Especially since these inequalities and inequities often affected workers doing the same work in the same plant, they undoubtedly took their toll in lessened collective consciousness. The efficacy of moral incentives would seem to depend on, among other things, considerable equality and equity in the sphere of material incentives. A New Person morality would be unlikely to fully develop when individuals see their sacrifices for the collectivity benefitting others more than themselves.

The material side of the *fidelista* incentive mix also undercut the development of collective consciousness by generating "socialist inflation," or incomes that outpaced available goods. After 1965, massive investments were made in agriculture, especially for future sugar output, and in cattle breeding. Such investments would result in increased output only over the long term. Investments were also heavy in collectively consumed services such as education, which was free and which would not pay off in increased output for many years. In addition, since most voluntary labor was paid at regular wages regardless of productivity, the sugar harvest, which used a considerable number of inexperienced volunteers, also helped generate socialist inflation. With prices held more or less constant, workers thus had considerably more money than there were goods or services on which to spend it.

If workers could not use their money for goods, many of them exchanged it for leisure, either by absenteeism or by low productivity on the job. In 1969, for example, the rate of absenteeism never fell below 35 percent for permanent farm workers in Camaguey Province. At the peak of the 1970 harvest, the final test of the New Person, the absentee rate for the whole economy reached 29 percent. In 1969, it was estimated that the agricultural labor force was utilized at somewhere around ''50 percent of practicable capacity.''[47]

It is impossible to judge the extent to which these problems resulted directly from the inadequate planning and administrative procedures of the *fidelista* model. But it seems reasonable to suppose that socialist inflation and the lack of a rational system of material sanctions and bonuses, both of which prevented harder work from paying off in increased personal consumption, played a significant role. Collective consciousness was developing unevenly. As many individuals made an effort to meet the goals and demands of the revolutionary leadership, others' work diminished. The fact that by 1968 voluntary work accounted for 8 to 10 percent of all labor indicated the efforts of some.[48] Absenteeism and low productivity indicated the backsliding of others.[49]

In 1970, Fidel Castro indicated the extent to which tension among workers had been engendered by the division between those who were expending great effort and those who were not. He remarked; ''Go to any factory and ask the workers what should be done about the lazy ones, the ones who don't work. If you don't watch out, they'll go so far as to demand that they be shot.''[50] Given the regime's own mistakes, which surely demoralized many a devoted worker, the term ''lazy ones'' may have simply blamed the victims. Be that as it may, the imbalanced incentive system, by allowing the lazy ones to effectively live off the labor of others, undoubtedly generated intra-working class resentments that further eroded the ability of collective and moral incentives to create greater collective consciousness. The *fidelista* incentive system undermined rather than encouraged the spread of the New Person.

Even beyond the tensions it engendered among workers, the *fidelista* implementation of the second development strategy eventually generated antagonisms between the revolutionary leadership and its political supporters in the working class. Workers could hardly fail to note that, through no fault of their own, much of their labor was being wasted. Many administrative personnel, on the other hand, did not recognize this. Instead, as a 1969 government report made clear, they tended to blame workers and took excessive coercive action against many of them.[51] This could only have added to workers' resentment and further strained relations between the leadership and its political base.

Moreover, the fact that in this period workers lacked institutionalized means for making suggestions, registering complaints, and venting resentments served to aggravate these tensions. Labor volunteers, for example, had little say about how their work was organized and few means to criticize the inefficient organizers of their projects. The *fidelista* antibureaucratic revolution had cut into the organizational apparatus of the unions, as well. The number of national unions dropped by almost half, down to 14, while their provincial and municipal branches were eliminated and unions across the board lost many of their former functions.[52] In Maurice Zeitlin's words, in the *fidelista* period the unions virtually "withered away."[53]

In addition, in this period the Party virtually took over the functions and organization of the state. It involved itself in the running of everything from the Academy of Sciences to the local grocery store. Enmeshed in day-to-day operations, the Party could not properly analyze problems and develop effective solutions. Because it had become the administration, it could not supervise and guide the administration, discover its mistakes, and make sure that it served the interests of the Cuban people. Most important, it could not even hope to represent the interests of the population before the administration.[54]

This is not to say the population had no way to make its voice heard in the *fidelista* period. They could, after all, speak with the revolutionary leadership, especially Fidel Castro, who routinely went about mixing with the people, querying them, listening to their criticisms, and then translating these into policy.[55] Given the uneven and episodic character of this sort of political participation, however, it is not surprising that increasing numbers of workers resorted to other mechanisms, once described by Che Guevara:

The State at times makes mistakes. When this occurs, the collective enthusiasm diminishes palpably as a result of the quantitative diminishing that takes place in each of the elements that make up the collective, and work becomes paralyzed until it finally shrinks to insignificant proportions: this is the time to rectify.[56]

Thus, in 1970 the Cuban revolution had reached a critical turning point. Educational advance had been impressive, but insufficient to adequately address the skill problem. The *fidelista* implementation of the second economic development strategy had failed to deliver the promised economic results. Moreover, it had left the administrative apparatus in shambles, filled with possibly professional revolutionaries but definitely amateur administrators. As will be seen in Chapter 5, many of these administrative personnel, with their few skills and often inefficient work styles, would retain administrative posts well into the future. Most immediately important, by 1970 the relationship between the revolutionary leadership and its popular political base showed definite signs of strain. The time to rectify had come.

NOTES

1. Good analyses of this first strategy and its failings can be found in Arthur MacEwan, *Revolution and Economic Development in Cuba* (New York: St. Martin's Press, 1981); and Archibald R. M. Ritter, *The Economic Development of Revolutionary Cuba* (New York: Praeger, 1974).

2. For full discussions of this second strategy, see ibid. and especially Heinrich Brunner, *Cuban Sugar Policy from 1963 to 1970* (Pittsburgh: University of Pittsburgh Press, 1977).

3. Leo Huberman and Paul Sweezy, *Socialism in Cuba* (New York: Monthly Review Press, 1969), p. 75.

4. MacEwan, *Revolution and Economic Development*, chaps. 13–21.

5. Slogans cited in Michel Huteau and Jacques Lautrey, *L'Éducation à Cuba* (Paris: François Maspero, 1973), p. 28.

6. Richard Fagen, *The Transformation of Political Culture in Cuba* (Stanford: Stanford University Press, 1969), p. 47.

7. UNCTAD, *Health and Education Technology in Cuba* (New York: United Nations Organization, 1979), p. 9. The campaign, of course, had a variety of results not indicated by these statistics. First, it whetted the appetite of many to raise their educational level, and thus prepared the way for the further expansion of the educational system. Second, the contact between urban and rural populations in the campaign helped to integrate Cuban society and to galvanize support for revolutionary goals. Third, the campaign gave regime officials experience in mobilizing and organizing the population on a broad scale. Fourth, the campaign allowed many youths who for one reason or another had not participated in the anti-Batista struggle to demonstrate and hone their leadership skills. On

these results, see MacEwan, *Revolution and Economic Development*, pp. 77–78; and Huteau and Lautrey, *L'Éducation à Cuba*, chap. 2.

8. Adult education in Cuba extends through the secondary level, and its graduates may go on to higher education while continuing in their regular jobs. Regular education begins with an extensive system of preprimary education; for a useful study, see Marvin Leiner, *Children Are the Revolution* (New York: Penguin Books, 1978). This is followed by an elementary educational system of six years (four years before the revolution) and a secondary educational system of up to eight years. After elementary school, students may enter one of three tracks of the basic secondary system: One track leads directly to production and continued secondary education in the adult system. Another track leads to a polytechnical school for two or three years of study and then to production and the adult system. The third track leads to three years of study in a basic secondary school. Graduates of the latter type of school may enter one of several tracks of the advanced secondary system: One track leads to production and the adult education system at the advanced secondary level. Another track leads to a polytechnical institute, either directly or after two or three years of study in an advanced polytechnical school, and then to higher education along with a regular job. Another track leads to a pedagogical school for four years and then to higher education. The last track leads to three years in a preuniversity and then either directly to higher education or to two years in a polytechnical institute and then to production or higher education. For a simplified flow chart of the Cuban educational system, see Francisco Ferreira Báez, "El sistema de formación profesional de nivel medio en Cuba," in Haydée García and Hans Blumenthal, eds., *Formación profesional en Latinoamerica* (Caracas: Editorial Nueva Sociedad, 1987), p. 115.

9. In fact, this battle was not won until 1980.

10. Reported by Carmelo Meso-Lago, *The Economy of Socialist Cuba* (Albuquerque: University of New Mexico Press, 1981), p. 164. Although the illiteracy figure may have risen due to changed statistical methodology, this probably cannot explain the whole increase.

11. Ministerio de Educación, *El plan de perfeccionamiento y desarrollo del Sistema Nacional de Educación de Cuba* (Havana: 1976), p. 63.

12. Ministerio de Educación, *Informe a la Asamblea Nacional del Poder Popular* (Havana: 1981), pp. 344–47.

13. UNCTAD, pp. 30–31; also see Consejo Superior de Universidades, *La reforma de la enseñanza superior en Cuba* (1962).

14. In fact, as late as 1974/75, the country still had only five higher education centers. See Concepción Duchesne, "Incremento y desarrollo en la educación superior, 1976–1980," *Bohemia*, Nov. 28, 1980, p. 36. The term "higher education centers" is used here rather than "universities" because, according to current Cuban nomenclature, the higher education system is made up of universities, university centers, and superior institutes. The latter two are generally smaller and more specialized than the universities. For a graphic representation

of the Cuban higher education system, see Nikolai Kolesnikov, *Cuba: educación popular y preparación de los cuadros nacionales, 1959–1982* (Moscow: Editorial Progreso, 1983), Anexo, Esquema 13.

15. For a detailed description of the ideological struggle in the university, written from a counterrevolutionary point of view, see Jaime Suchlicki, *University Students and Revolution in Cuba, 1920–1968* (Coral Gables: University of Miami Press, 1968), Chapter 5.

16. See "Estudio preliminar sobre algunos factores que inciden en las realizaciones docentes de los alumnos de primer año," *Sobre Educación Superior* (1971), pp. 43–50; and Guillermo Aria and Arturo Bas, "Construcción de un instrumento adecuado para evaluar a los estudiantes que ingresar a la universidad," *Sobre Educación Superior* (1971), pp. 51–65.

17. Author's interviews BFG01.81 and BFG02.81.

18. Consejo Superior de Universidades, *La reforma*.

19. Author's interview ST.80.

20. See, for example, Ministerio de Educación, *Informe de la delegación de la República de Cuba a la VII Conferencia de Ministros de Educación Superior y Media Especializada de los Países Socialistas* (Havana: 1972), p. 82.

21. Depending on the context, I have translated the Spanish term *economía* as either "economic studies" or "economy," instead of "economics." Also, I have used the term "economic professionals" to refer to professional economists (*economistas*), but not solely to them. The reason for these choices is that the distinction between economic studies and what in the United States would be called business studies is less complete in Cuba than it is in the United States. Cuban economic studies programs, for example, commonly train not just professional economists but also accountants, managers, etc. Moreover, in Cuba all economic professionals, whether or not they are professional economists, are eligible for membership in the National Association of Cuban Economic Professionals (Asociación Nacional de Economistas de Cuba). In Cuba, then, it makes sense to speak of economic professionals as a single category.

Unless otherwise indicated, the information in this chapter on economic professionals in Cuba is taken from Alexis Codina Jiménez and Joaquín Fernández, "Apuntes en el XX aniversario del inicio de la formación de economistas," *Economía y Desarrollo* 71 (Nov.-Dec. 1982), pp. 11–37.

22. See Nikolai Bukharin, *The Economics of the Transformation Period* (New York: Bergman, 1971); and Rosa Luxemburg, "What Is Economics?" in Mary-Alice Waters, ed., *Rosa Luxemburg Speaks* (New York: Pathfinder Press, 1970), pp. 219–45.

23. Osvaldo Dorticós, "Formación de cuadros economicos-administrativos en la industria ligera," *Economía y Desarrollo* 4 (Oct.-Dec. 1970), pp. 3–8.

24. For this debate and the economic models it counterposed, see the collection by Bertram Silverman, ed., *Man and Socialism in Cuba: The Great Debate* (New York: Atheneum, 1973).

25. Ernesto "Che" Guevara, "On the Budgetary Finance System," in ibid., p. 152.

26. Ernesto "Che" Guevara, "Against Bureaucratism," in John Gerassi, ed., *Venceremos! The Speeches and Writings of Che Guevara* (New York: Simon and Schuster, 1968), p. 224.

27. Nelson P. Valdés, "The Cuban Revolution: Economic Organization and Bureaucracy," *Latin American Perspectives*, issue 20 (Winter 1979), pp. 13–37.

28. Perhaps the most representative statements are by Ernesto "Che" Guevara, "Man and Socialism in Cuba," in Silverman, *Man and Socialism in Cuba*, pp. 337–354; and Fidel Castro, "We Will Never Build a Communist Consciousness with a Dollar Sign in the Minds and Hearts of Men," in Martin Kenner and James Petras, eds., *Fidel Castro Speaks* (New York: Grove Press, 1969), pp. 199–213.

29. Fidel Castro, *Fidel in Chile* (New York: International Publishers, 1975), p. 185.

30. My interpretation of Guevara's meaning thus differs from that of MacEwan, *Revolution and Economic Development*, p. 108, who says, "Guevara's assertions . . . that a necessary connection existed between the structure of planning and the structure of incentives are difficult to maintain. There is no reason, in theory, why it is not possible to have decentralization combined with political or collective motivation." MacEwan is, of course, correct from a strictly economic point of view, but Guevara, while keenly aware of and concerned with the economics of his position, was equally concerned with the social implications of his model. It is the latter that explains why he felt that the system of moral and collective incentives required a centralized structure of planning and economic organization. Without centralization, the economy would be fractured into a multitude of competing groups at the ministerial, enterprise, and work center levels. This objective structure would undercut the attempt to create collective consciousness through the incentive system. From the Guevarist point of view, it was the decentralized model that was theoretically confused, for its objective structure contradicted the desire to instill in each individual the subjective awareness of being part of a single whole, for which one worked and to which one needed to be responsible. For an interpretation of Guevara's thought that is consistent with the above, see Carlos Tablada, *Che Guevara: Economics and Politics in the Transition to Socialism* (Sydney, Australia: Pathfinder/Pacific and Asia, 1989).

31. For example, Valdés, "The Cuban Revolution," p. 17.

32. For example, René Dumont, *Cuba: Est-il Socialiste?* (Paris: Éditions du Seuil, 1970).

33. "The Struggle Against Bureaucracy: A Decisive Task," in Michael Taber, ed., *Fidel Castro Speeches, Vol. 2: Our Power Is that of the Working People* (New York: Pathfinder Press, 1983), pp. 68–90. Although not the first attempt in the 1960s to cut the size of the administrative apparatus, this was the most radical.

34. Ibid., p. 86.

35. See, for example, the cover to the paperback edition of K. S. Karol, *Guerrillas in Power: The Course of the Cuban Revolution* (New York: Hill and Wang, 1970).

36. Dorticós, "Formación," pp. 3–8.

37. This can also be seen in the *fidelista* Revolutionary Offensive of 1968, mentioned earlier. The difference was that the Revolutionary Offensive struck against the small proprietor sector of the intermediate strata, especially in commerce.

The perception of the prerevolutionary intermediate strata as politically unreliable dates at least to the regimes of Ramón Grau San Martín and Carlos Prío Socorrás. When these petty bourgeois nationalists held the presidency between 1944 and 1952, they shamed themselves and their supporters in the eyes of the Cuban masses. Of Grau, Hugh Thomas has accurately said, "Trampling on the expectations of many people who placed faith in his promises, he did a great disservice to the cause of democratic reform. . . . His period of power is appropriately commemorated by the career of a minor official at the Ministry of Education, who arrived in Miami . . . after two years as minister with $M20 in notes in his suitcase, not to speak of thousands of caballerias of land, sugar mills, air companies and a chain of houses left behind." Hugh Thomas, *Cuba: The Pursuit of Freedom* (New York: Harper and Row, 1971), pp. 757–58.

38. For example, Claes Brundenius, *Revolutionary Cuba: The Challenge of Economic Growth with Equity* (Boulder, CO.: Westview Press, 1984), p. 40, gives estimates from which it can be computed that, from 1966 through 1970, total material product grew at an average annual rate of 3.72 percent, gross material product at 0.4 percent, gross domestic product at 0.68 percent, and gross domestic product per capita at -1.14 percent. For the planned rate quoted in the text, see Carlos Rafael Rodríguez, cited in Ritter, *Economic Development of Revolutionary Cuba*, p. 316; and for Castro's report of the actual rate, see Fidel Castro, *Main Report to the First Congress of the Communist Party of Cuba* (Havana: Communist Party of Cuba, 1977).

39. MacEwan, *Revolution and Economic Development*, p. 117.

40. Ritter, *Economic Development of Revolutionary Cuba*, pp. 183–87.

41. According to data given to me in 1981 by Eugenio Balari, Director of the Cuban Institute of Internal Demand, the average daily per capita caloric intake in 1970 was 2,565, almost 400 calories short of the 2,940 considered necessary for the average Cuban. Daily per capita protein intake in the same year was 68.8 grams, about 20 grams short of the necessary 89.

42. Ritter, *Economic Development of Revolutionary Cuba*, pp. 287–88. Also consult the complaints of the workers at the *Cubano de Acero* factory in *Granma Weekly Review*, Sept. 2, 1973.

43. Quoted in Maurice Zeitlin, *Revolutionary Politics and the Cuban Working Class* (Princeton, NJ: Princeton University Press, 1967), p. xxii.

44. See the remarks of Fidel Castro in Martin Kenner and James Petras, *Fidel Castro Speaks*, p. 288; and Karol, *Guerrillas in Power*, p. 343. According to

Castro, the rationale for this policy was the probable negative political consequences of the government's lowering wages, even if only the highest ones.

45. Karol, *Guerrillas in Power*, p. 338.

46. Eduardo DeLlano, "Wages under Socialism," *Granma Weekly Review*, Nov. 25, 1973.

47. Huberman and Sweezy, *Socialism in Cuba*, p. 143.

48. Carmelo Mesa-Lago, "Economic Significance of Unpaid Labor in Socialist Cuba," *Industrial and Labor Relations Review* 22 (April 1969), pp. 339–57.

49. Thus, it would be as wrong to argue that moral incentives are in themselves unworkable as it would be to argue that they automatically lead to collective consciousness. To accomplish the latter task, moral incentives need to be balanced with a rational and equitable system of material incentives. For the universal development of the New Person, attitudes must change. But in the early stages of socialist transition, when collective consciousness is still unevenly distributed, the key problem would seem to be behavioral. Those who do not respond to moral incentives need to be encouraged to put forth a degree of productive effort that at least approaches that of their more conscientious coworkers. Without a balanced incentive system, which ensures equality or equity in distribution and at the same time elicits equal or equitable amounts of productive effort, collective consciousness will be undermined. The argument that moral incentives are in themselves unworkable has been suggested by Carmelo Mesa-Lago, *Cuba in the 1970s* (Albuquerque: University of New Mexico Press, 1974). The opposite argument for collective (moral) incentives, has been suggested by Arthur MacEwan, "Incentives, Equality, and Power in Cuba," in Ronald Radosh, ed., *The New Cuba* (New York: Morrow, 1976), pp. 74–101. Neither of these approaches appreciates the dialectical interplay of the material and moral sides of the incentive mix. Both focus solely on equality/inequality in distribution, and both ignore equality/inequality in productive effort. Mac-Ewan, in *Revolution and Economic Development*, has moved over to the dialectical understanding of the question. For further comments on this, see Frank T. Fitzgerald, "Cuba and the Problem of Socialist Development," *Monthly Review*, 33, 11 (April 1982), pp. 48–51.

50. Fidel Castro, "Report on the Cuban Economy," in Rolando Bonachea and Nelson Valdés, eds., *Cuba in Revolution* (Garden City, NY: Doubleday, 1972), p. 341.

51. *Granma Weekly Review*, Nov. 9, 1969.

52. Linda Fuller, "The Politics of Workers' Control in Cuba, 1959–1983: The Work Center and the National Arena" (Ph.D. diss., University of California at Berkeley, 1985), pp. 134–36.

53. Zeitlin, *Revolutionary Politics*, p. xxxiii.

54. See the discussion of these points in Lourdes Casal, "Cuban Communist Party: The Best among the Good," *Cuba Review*, 6, 3 (Sept. 1976), p. 24.

55. For a graphic illustration of this, see Lee Lockwood, *Castro's Cuba, Cuba's Fidel* (New York: Vintage Books, 1969).

56. Guevara, "Man and Socialism in Cuba," pp. 339–40.

4

The Post–1970 Rectification Process

Cuban socialism underwent a profound rectification in the 1970s.[1] Economically, the revolutionary leadership pursued less ambitious goals and a more balanced development strategy. Although a variety of economic problems remained, the annual growth rate in gross domestic product averaged an estimated 7.8 percent during the ten years from 1972 through 1981, while the per capita rate averaged 6.5 percent.[2] Agricultural production reportedly grew a moderate 27 percent in the decade from 1970 to 1980, while greater emphasis was put on industry, which grew 80 percent.[3]

The post–1970 rectification process also jettisoned the *fidelista* system. The leadership attempted to introduce a more balanced incentive system and to institutionalize new organizational structures and operating procedures, designed to overcome the strains of the late 1960s and to resolidify the leadership's popular base. The new organizational principles, as will be seen, called for an increasing number of formally trained personnel, that is, for new professionals. They also called for the conversion or replacement of those who had risen in the 1960s to intermediate-level posts on the basis of political credentials, who could now in the 1970s be called the old cadres, as the minimum qualification for entry into these occupations officially became a secondary school degree. Finally, in line with the above, the educational system was rectified to decisively address the skill problem and to increase the supply of new professionals.

THE NEW ORGANIZATIONAL PRINCIPLES

The post–1970 rectification process was partly aimed at institutionalizing new organizational structures, with differentiated areas and levels of responsibility. The major economic and political organizations were to be given formally delineated spheres of responsibility, as were the hierarchy of levels within these organizations. Although, at least in its formal, structural aspects, akin to Max Weber's ideal-typical rational bureaucratic model, this new organizational setup was not to operate solely along the monocratic, nondemocratic lines of Weber's model.[4] Instead, its operating procedures were to encompass an element of bottom-up participation, which Weber, of course, considered alien to his model. The new structures were supposed to operate according to a three-step "democratic centralist" process for making and implementing decisions.[5]

In the first step of this process, the issue at hand is to be collectively discussed. Here, intermediate-level personnel and, at the local level, the general population are to be involved in analyzing problems and in examining and proposing possible solutions. Failure to adequately carry through this step is said to lead to less than optimal decisions, in that such decisions will ignore realities of which only lower bodies have full knowledge, and to "bureaucratic centralist" decisions, in that lower bodies will lack identification with such decisions, which will then have to be imposed from above.

In the second step of the democratic centralist process, a decision is to be made. This responsibility is assigned to leaders of enterprises, of work centers (local subunits of enterprises), of mass organizations, or of higher Party and state organs. More general or more important decisions are to be made by higher-level leaders, while less general or less important decisions are to be reserved for lower-level leaders. Allowing decisions to be made at too low a level is said to lead to local improvisation, waste of resources, and inattention to internal and external factors beyond the purview of lower bodies, or, in short, to less than optimal decisions. Allowing decisions to be made at too high a level is said to be bureaucratic centralist, in the sense that the higher levels will thereby be usurping responsibilities of lower-level leaders.

In the third step, the active participation of the lower levels, down to the localities, is to be elicited in the implementation and control of these decisions, that is, in ensuring that they are carried out fully and correctly according to plan. Participation is to be encouraged through persuasion, especially through fully explaining the rationale for the particular decisions made. Failure to elicit lower-level participation through persuasion and explanation is also dubbed bureaucratic centralist, in that lower level compliance and cooperation will then have to be commanded from above.[6]

The principles of democratic centralism define a particular distribution of decision-making power, one that points to the increased importance of the new professionals. First, these principles stipulate that the most general or societal decisions should be made centrally, that is, by the revolutionary leadership. Although this reserves ultimate decision-making responsibility for the leadership itself, it does not preclude the leadership from eliciting the advice of trained specialists from among the new professionals.

Second, democratic centralist principles stipulate that, although people at the local level should not make decisions, they should participate in the pre-decision-making stage of discussion and in the post-decision-making stage of implementation. Thus, democratic centralism envisions eliciting and solidifying popular support for decisions made at higher levels through participatory mechanisms, however limited.

Third, these principles stipulate that less general or less important decisions should be left to lower-level administrative personnel. If decisions made at this level are to be optimal, lower-level decision makers, of course, must possess skills adequate to their responsibilities. In this way, the principles of democratic centralism implicitly call for and justify the replacement of old cadres by new professionals.

The principles of democratic centralism, then, define the distribution of decision-making power. They justify the subordination of the new professionals to the leadership, but they also justify the rise of the new professionals to replace the old cadres. In addition, these principles justify for the new professionals a clear and stable intermediate-level role in the rectified organizational structures. Overall, the principles of democratic centralism define and justify the distribution of decision-making power, call for limited popular participation, and increase the demand for new professionals.

RECTIFYING ECONOMIC ORGANIZATION AND INCENTIVES

Among the first organizational structures to be institutionalized according to the principles of democratic centralism after 1970 were the trade unions, which, as already noted, had virtually withered away in the late 1960s. From 1970 to 1972, the unions were reorganized into 23 national unions in the various sectors of the economy, and were equipped with the provincial and municipal organizational levels that had been stripped away in 1966.[7] This reconstruction of the trade unions culminated in the Thirteenth Congress of the Central Organization of Cuban Trade Unions (CTC), held in 1973.

One major accomplishment of this congress was to clarify the role of the unions. As mass organizations to which all workers could belong, the unions were to be considered separate from both Party and state. The division between the unions and the Party, however, would be functional rather than political. Unions were to function as "transmission belts," both up and down, between the Party and the mass of workers. Because workers constitute only a part of the population, their unions were not empowered to control the management of the economy. Rather, they were expected to follow the ideological lead of the Party, as the vanguard organization of the whole society. Yet, as one labor leader put it, "The trade unions are not going every day to the Party to ask what has to be done. Their function is to develop, along the fundamentals of the Party line, the administration of the trade unions."[8]

However vague the actual power delegated to the unions, this partial differentiation of the responsibilities of the unions from those of the Party and the state paved the way for the differentiation of the functions of the unions and the enterprise and work center (local subunits of enterprises) management. As the organizational voice of the particular interests of the workers, the unions were now expected to point out errors in the work and planning process and to help organize workers' participation. Workers were to be involved in discussing the basic production issues and in controlling the implementation of the economic plan of their enterprise and work center. Although managers would continue to be appointed from above and be considered ultimately responsible for the overall performance of their economic unit, union representatives were not to side indiscriminately with management, as many had in the past.[9] As the statutes approved by the Thirteenth CTC Congress put it, the trade unions were to play a counterpart or, perhaps more accurately, a countervailing role (un papel contrapartida) in relation to management, and were to actively criticize all manifestations of managerial inefficiency, as well as protect workers' rights.[10]

A second major accomplishment of the Thirteenth CTC Congress was to officially promulgate the principle of "to each according to work." This signified that the fidelista incentive system would be replaced by a more balanced mixture of moral and material incentives. Moral incentives would still be used, but less extensively than in the late 1960s. Material incentives would increase in importance, but they would be more carefully related to productivity. Moreover, the greater distributional inequality that would result was to be kept within fairly strict bounds. As will be seen in Chapter 7, revolutionary leaders have suggested that the balance in the incentive system began to break down in 1980, when certain limits on the use of material incentives were lifted. But through the 1970s a rough balance seems to have been maintained.

After 1970, a variety of moral incentives continued to be used. First, beginning in 1971 many important consumer goods, especially durables, were distributed so as to make their purchase much less dependent on an individual's income. Refrigerators, TV sets, sewing machines, and other consumer durables were distributed to those workers with the greatest need and the best work records as judged by general workers' meetings or by union committees.[11]

Second, symbolic rewards continued to be granted for successful "socialist emulation." After 1973, individuals could compete with others to become Vanguard Workers by exceeding work norms, conserving raw materials, observing work discipline, passing adult education courses, and participating in voluntary labor. In addition, work centers designated exemplary were allowed to fly the Banner of the Heroes of Moncada.

Third, although voluntary labor tapered off in the sugar sector, it continued to be used elsewhere. To enable voluntary laborers to see the material benefits of their presumably morally motivated efforts, after 1970 the resources realized on so-called Red Sundays and other special days were devoted to the construction of some highly visible facility for the whole society, such as a school or hospital.[12] Beginning in 1971, work centers volunteered to form "microbrigades" to construct housing and other facilities. Microbrigade volunteers received their regular pay, while the comrades left behind in their work center compensated for their absence with unpaid overtime, or "plus-work." This system flourished until 1980, when, for reasons that will be discussed in Chapter 7, it fell into disuse.

To reemphasize material incentives after 1970, payment according to work norms was formally reintroduced. Bonuses of various sorts were granted for overfulfillment of norms, and wage cuts were instituted for underfulfillment. Overtime pay, which had been widely renounced in the late 1960s, was also reintroduced. Finally, in 1980, a far-reaching General Wage Reform was promulgated.

For a minority of the labor force, this reform reduced present and possible future wages by formally outlawing historical and other out-of-line wages, and by reducing the maximum wage for agricultural workers, as industrial development received increased emphasis. For the majority of the labor force, however, this reform increased wages. First, it increased the minimum wage for all categories of workers. Second, it increased the importance of bonuses by allowing them to be a larger proportion of the actual wage paid. Third, it increased the maximum wage for nonagricultural service and office workers, and for technical and managerial personnel. In addition, official wage scales for technicians and managers were stretched from twelve to twenty categories, matching the remuneration for these groups with levels of responsibility and educational preparation. Although individuals without the requisite educational credentials could still be hired as technicians and managers, they would now have to be placed at the minimum wage level and could advance up the wage scale only as they acquired the requisite formal education. In these ways, the General Wage Reform favored the new professionals.[13]

To ensure that material incentives would elicit greater productive effort, opportunities for consumption were increased. In the first half of the 1970s, socialist inflation was virtually eliminated, and the amount and diversity of consumer goods was increased. Although essential items continued to be rationed, between 1970 and 1980 the types of products rationed fell from 94 to 21 percent of all types of consumer goods.[14] A "parallel market," offering goods at official but higher prices, was introduced.[15] Furthermore, beginning in 1980, the revolutionary leadership began to relax some of the restrictions on small-scale private enterprise that it had imposed in the Revolutionary Offensive of 1968. Private repair and other services were allowed and licensed. So-called free farmers' markets were opened, where farmers could sell a certain amount of their produce at whatever price the market would bear.[16] In 1984, a General Law on Housing was promulgated that, among other things, allowed individuals to construct, sell, and rent housing at free market prices.[17]

Consistent with the reemphasis on material incentives, a new Economic Management and Planning System (Sistema de Dirección y Planificación de la Economía—SDPE), similar to the auto-finance system of the early 1960s, was gradually introduced.[18] Under study as early as 1973, the SDPE was officially promulgated in 1975. Its planning aspect was introduced immediately, and its management aspect was gradually introduced beginning in 1978 and extended to the whole economy by the early 1980s.[19]

As early as 1969, then President Osvaldo Dorticós pointed out that multi-level and long-range planning and management, such as was entailed by the introduction of the SDPE, required a significant increase in the number of trained, new professional economic and managerial personnel.[20] On the one hand, these were needed to formulate, implement, adjust, and evaluate plans. On the other, they were needed to manage day-to-day operations at all levels of the new economic system. In contrast to the *fidelista* system, which in the late 1960s had sent both economic professionals and economic controls "to the garbage pail,"[21] the SDPE reintroduced economic controls and increased the demand for trained economic controllers.

The SDPE envisioned an elaborate planning process that would involve central planning authorities,[22] sectoral and regional officials, and ministry, enterprise, and work center managers and workers.[23] No longer would Cuban planning be limited to annual or even shorter range plans. In 1975, the first five-year plan was introduced. And in 1980, the first twenty-year plan, which was to be updated every five years, was announced.

Under SDPE, the final plan is not supposed to determine the obligations of enterprises and work centers in detail. Instead, the plan merely determines key indicators, such as amount of physical output, average number of workers, amount of raw materials, and average level of productivity. Operating within these and centrally fixed prices for materials, labor, and output, SDPE enterprises are supposed to be cost-accounting units, with profit (receipts minus costs at planned prices) and profitability (the profit/capital ratio) serving as their main performance criteria. Exactly how these criteria are met, however, is supposed to be largely left up to the enterprises themselves, which are formally envisioned as semi-autonomous units.

SDPE enterprises are also supposed to have financial autonomy, with the right to maintain a bank account that no other organization can utilize. They can apply to the National Bank for loans, which are supposed to be paid back with interest in timely fashion. The National Bank is thus supposed to exercise financial control over SDPE enterprises, by denying further credit to those that fail in their payments. This, of course, is meant to encourage enterprises to operate efficiently.

In general, SDPE enterprises are supposed to realize a profit to maintain their credit rating, but also to accomplish a variety of other tasks. For example, SDPE enterprises are expected to pay a depreciation tax for the use of the basic means of production supplied to them by the state. They can also be held legally responsible for late deliveries, shoddy goods, failure to abide by contracts with other enterprises, and other malfeasance; and the fines that they may be required to pay are supposed to come from their profits. Ultimately, SDPE enterprises are supposed to realize a profit in order to finance the material incentive funds that constitute an important motive force of the whole system. A sociocultural fund is to pay for such things as housing, day care centers, and dining halls for the enterprise labor force. Another fund is for rewarding enterprise personnel with personal and collective bonuses, in accordance with performance.[24] If the SDPE enterprise does not produce efficiently, does not realize a profit, does not meet its financial and other obligations, then it is not supposed to be allowed to set up and disburse these incentive funds, and it is supposed to lose one of its main mechanisms of labor force motivation.

The introduction of the SDPE was supposed to make workers and managers materially responsible for their own economic performance and for that of their work center and enterprise. It was supposed to make all economically active individuals more economically conscious. And it was supposed to more closely integrate their individual interests with the collective interest of their enterprise and with the social interest of the whole economy. But the SDPE has not yet lived up to these expectations, and by 1986 some of its aspects discussed above were at least temporarily jettisoned. As will be explained in Chapter 6, the SDPE's problems have had many causes, but, at least in part, they have stemmed from the behavior of the old cadres, although leaders, workers, and new professionals have played a part as well.

RECTIFYING POLITICAL ORGANIZATIONS

The post–1970 rectification process also set up a new democratic centralist form of participation in the administration of the state, the Organs of Popular Power (Organos de Poder Popular—OPP). This formally divides state responsibilities among national, provincial, and municipal offices that are overseen by bodies of elected representatives. Begun on an experimental basis in Matanzas Province in 1974, approved by the First Party Congress in 1975, and codified in the new Cuban Constitution in 1976, the OPP were extended across the island during 1976–1977.[25]

Production and service units, depending on which area they primarily serve, are overseen by the national, provincial, or municipal OPPs. A municipal OPP, for example, might oversee local units such as schools, theaters, health facilities, factories, and restaurants.[26] Neither the municipal nor provincial OPPs, however, have unrestricted rein over the units assigned to them. They cannot, for example, introduce their own schedule of prices, wages, school curricula, or statistical procedures. Such norms, procedures, and methods are determined by central authorities, formally subordinated to the national OPP assembly. This assembly, according to the new Cuban Constitution, is "the only organ in the Republic invested with constituent and legislative authority."[27] As such, the national OPP assembly approves all laws, national economic plans, national budgets, and other nationwide legislation.

The OPPs at all levels are charged with helping overcome economic inefficiencies and to improve the delivery of goods and services to the population. To accomplish these ends, the OPPs can appoint the management of the economic units under their jurisdiction and can impose a variety of sanctions if necessary. Moreover, to help in these matters, all OPP assemblies have administrative staff that together make up the organizational apparatus of the Cuban state. While OPP delegates may be amateurs, if they are to effectively carry out their oversight functions, they require a staff of trained personnel. Thus, the creation of OPPs has increased the demand for new professionals.

The OPPs are constituted from the municipal level upward.[28] After neighborhoods have nominated at least two candidates for each available seat in the municipal OPP assembly, biographies of each candidate are circulated among the electors, the only form of "campaigning" that is allowed. The neighborhood voters that make up a constituency then elect by secret ballot one of the candidates as their delegate to the municipal OPP. The municipal delegates then elect the delegates to both the provincial and national OPP assemblies, from slates presented by nominating committees, composed of representatives of mass and political organizations and chaired by a representative of the Party.[29] These committees must in most instances nominate at least 25 percent more candidates than available seats, and electors may reject the committees' slates in whole or in part. Finally, again from slates presented by nominating committees, the municipal and provincial OPP assemblies elect their own executive committees, while the National Assembly elects the Council of Ministers and the Council of State.

The OPP system has a variety of mechanisms to ensure participation from the bottom up, and to enable it to transmit decisions, information, suggestions, and complaints both up and down between the revolutionary leadership and the rest of the population. OPP delegates at all levels, for example, are required to report periodically to their electors in formal "rendering of accounts" meetings. In these, delegates are obliged to report on their activities and on the pressing issues before their OPP, and the electors are encouraged to raise their own issues. If the questions and concerns of the electors cannot be answered or resolved at the time, OPP delegates are required to present a satisfactory answer or resolution at the next regular accounts meeting. In addition, the OPP system provides for the recall of delegates and the election of new ones at the pleasure of the majority of electors. Overall, the OPP system supplies the population with a channel for voicing complaints and seeking to solve problems, especially at the local level. Certainly, the OPP system gives the revolutionary leadership a communication channel to alert it to popular concerns before they reach crisis proportions, as they did in the late 1960s.

But ultimately the domination of the revolutionary leadership and of its societal decisions is secured by the nomination and election procedures of the OPP system. This system gives the revolutionary leadership considerable control over who can be nominated, and therefore elected, to higher OPP posts. Not surprisingly, then, since the system's inception, an overwhelming majority of delegates to the higher OPP assemblies have been members of the Communist Party or of the Union of Young Communists.[30]

It is through these that the revolutionary leadership exercises control over the most important OPP decisions. As Raúl Castro explained:

The Party does not administer. . . . The Party can and must take suggestions, proposals, recommendations; it must counsel and guide the organs of People's Power, but must never "hand down decisions," never impose decisions, never undertake any manner of reprisal as regards an organ of People's Power or members of such organs who do not agree with or will not carry out something the Party has suggested, proposed, recommended, advised, or set down in a guideline. The Party must use, as its principal means to guarantee that its guidelines and criteria are put into practice by the organs of People's Power, the work of the Party members who are also delegates to those organs or members of executive committees. Party members . . . are obliged to comply with and carry out the decisions of the Party and to convince . . . the non-Party members of the fairness of those decisions and the need to apply them. If, after exhausting all the methods and resources within their authority . . . the Party leadership at a given level . . . does not convince the organs of People's Power at that level to follow a recommendation or guideline that it considers important, it must then refer to the next highest level of the Party . . . to discuss the matter at . . . [its] level of People's Power.[31]

In other words, the Party is not to directly administer the state or to command the decisions of non-Party OPP delegates. But Party members in OPP posts remain under Party discipline and are obliged to attempt to persuade the other OPP delegates to follow the Party line. If this fails at the lower levels, then matters are to be taken to the next higher OPP level, where many more delegates will be Party members, and where, as a consequence, conformity with the Party line will ultimately be assured.

Raúl Castro's stricture against direct Party administration reflects another aspect of the post–1970 reactification process. Unlike in the 1960s, the Party is now officially defined as an organization limited to persuasion for setting its stamp on state and society.[32] In fact, the partial removal of the Party from direct administration has opened space for other organizations, including trade unions, economic units, and OPPs, to operate semi-autonomously. Still, these organizations remain ultimately controlled by the revolutionary leadership. This happens not only through the mechanisms described by Raúl Castro for the OPP, but also directly through the *nomenclature*, a list of posts that the Party retains the exclusive right to fill with candidates of its choice.[33] There is no way to know how many of these posts are intermediate-level or who these candidates are. But given the leadership's post–1970 policy of favoring new professionals over old cadres, whatever intermediate posts have been involved have probably routinely gone to new professionals.

RECTIFYING THE EDUCATIONAL SYSTEM

The changes in economic and political structures after 1970 were paralleled by changes in education. Rectifying the educational system to address decisively the shortage of skills and increase the supply of new professionals began in the 1970/71 school year. Then, in the reconstruction of the trade unions, teachers in every school and cultural workers in every province met to "analyze and debate the principal problems of education."[34] From these meetings arose a new National Union of Educational Workers; the First National Congress of Education and Culture was held in Havana in April 1971. Out of this congress, whose almost eighteen hundred delegates generated over three thousand recommendations, came a directive to the Ministry of Education to undertake a diagnostic study of Cuban education at all levels. This study, begun in the 1972/73 school year, resulted in a plan (El Plan de Perfeccionamiento y Desarrollo del Sistema Nacional de Educación de Cuba) for improving and developing the educational system at all levels, which was approved by the First Congress of the Party and by the Ministry of Education in 1975.[35]

As a result of this renewed attention, the educational system expanded more rapidly and surely than in the 1960s. Enrollments in the adult education system expanded consistently from 316,896 in 1970/71 to 701,259 in 1976/77 (see Table 4.1). The tapering off of these enrollments between 1977/78 and 1980/81 was probably due to success rather than failure. Adult illiteracy had reportedly been reduced to 4.0 percent by 1980 and to 1.9 percent of the twenty-to-forty-nine-year-old population

Table 4.1

Adult, Primary, Secondary, and Higher Education Enrollments in Cuba, 1970/71 to 1984/85

School Year	Enrollment			
	Adult	Primary	Secondary	Higher [a]
1970/71	316,896	1,530,376	272,193	35,137
1971/72	326,048	1,631,187	282,279	36,877
1972/73	398,048	1,733,208	324,401	48,735
1973/74	445,798	1,780,775	395,544	55,435
1974/75	413,847	1,801,191	520,295	68,051
1975/76	597,596	1,795,752	629,197	83,957
1976/77	701,259	1,747,738	806,049	110,148
1977/78	605,247	1,693,942	963,304	131,547
1978/79	580,880	1,626,386	1,074,286	146,293
1979/80	391,990	1,550,323	1,150,372	200,288
1980/81	277,003	1,468,538	1,177,813	205,000
1981/82	342,700	1,409,800	1,182,600	200,000
1982/83	392,900	1,363,100	1,116,900	200,000
1983/84	393,700	1,283,000	1,140,900	222,200
1984/85	N.A.	N.A.	N.A.	240,000

Sources: For adult, primary, and secondary education from 1970/71 through 1980/81, Ministerio de Educación, Informe a la Asamblea Nacional del Poder Popular (Havana: 1981), pp. 344-346; for 1981/82 through 1983/84, Ministerio de Educación, Organización de la educación 1981-1983, informe a la XXXIX Conferencia Internacional de Educación, Ginebra, Suiza 1984 (Havana: 1984), p. 173. For higher education from 1970/71 through 1979/80, Ministerio de Educación, Informe, pp. 344-346; for 1980/81, Elena Díaz González, "La mujer y necesdades humanas básicas," Economía y Desarrollo, 64 (Sept.-Oct. 1981), p. 219; for 1981/82 through 1983/84, Ministerio de Educación, Organización, p. 173; for 1984/85, Federación de Mujeres Cubanas, Cuban Women in Higher Education (Havana: Editorial Letras Cubanas, 1985), p. 22.

a. Includes all university-level day, evening, and correspondence courses.

"able to study" by 1981.[36] In 1980, the Cubans declared victory in the "Battle for the Sixth Grade" and in the struggle for the ninth grade by 1985.[37]

Primary school enrollments rose to a high of 1,801,191 in 1974/75 and then gradually declined (see Table 4.1). By 1983/84, there were almost one-quarter million fewer students enrolled at the primary level than in 1970/71, and a 28.8 percent drop from the peak year, 1974/75. The steady drop in primary level enrollments in the second half of the 1970s and the early 1980s was due to both demographic change and improved efficiency. On the one hand, primary-level enrollment dropped as the birth rate slowed. The birth rate, which had been 26.1 per thousand in 1958, soared to 35.1 per thousand by 1963 with the initial revolutionary improvements in living conditions and health care, but then began a steady decline to 15.8 per thousand by 1979.[38] That it is this declining birth rate that explains the decline in primary school enrollments and not a falling-off of primary school enrollment efforts is evident given that, between 1974/75 and 1980/81, the percentage of the six-to-twelve-year-old age cohort attending school actually rose from 98.4 to 98.8 percent.[39]

Declining primary school enrollments also resulted from improved efficiency. As mentioned earlier, of the class that entered first grade in 1964 and was scheduled to complete sixth grade in 1970, only 20.7 percent were graduated on time.[40] In 1981, however, 70.8 percent of the primary-level students who had begun in 1975 were successfully graduated.[41]

Although both adult and primary education recovered from some of the problems they had experienced in the late 1960s and scored new successes after 1970, it was in secondary and higher education that enrollments expanded most dramatically. As primary-level enrollments dropped from 83.3 percent of total enrollments in 1970/71 to 48.5 percent in 1983/84, secondary enrollments went from 14.8 to 43.1 percent, and higher education, from 1.9 to 8.4 percent (see Table 4.2).

In part, the astounding expansion of secondary education after 1970 was made possible by improvements at the primary level, which now readied greater numbers of students to enter secondary grades, just as the expansion of higher education resulted from improvements at the secondary level. In addition, the emphasis put on higher education in this period allowed many more to undertake their university training at a younger age. This new emphasis was symbolized perhaps most clearly by the creation in 1977 of a separate Ministry of Higher Education.[42]

But the change in the structure of total enrollments was also the result of the post–1970 rectification of major economic and political institutions that increased the demand for trained personnel—the new professionals—for intermediate-level occupations. In the 1970s, the policy of coopting personnel into these occupations primarily on the basis of political credentials was stopped. The minimum qualification for entry into these occupations officially became a secondary school degree. Thus, supplying

Table 4.2

Primary, Secondary, and Higher Education Enrollments as a Percentage of Total Enrollments in Cuba, 1970/71 and 1983/84

School Year	Enrollment			
	Primary	Secondary	Higher	Total
1970/71	83.3%	14.8%	1.9%	100.0%
1983/84	48.5	43.1	8.4	100.0

Sources: Author's computations based, for 1970/71, on Ministerio de Educación, Informe a la Asamblea Nacional del Poder Popular (Havana: 1981), pp. 344-347; for 1983/84, Ministerio de Educación, Organización de la educación 1981-1983, informe a la XXXIX Conferencia Internacional de Educación, Ginebra, Suiza 1984 (Havana: 1984), p. 173.

sufficient numbers of new professionals required expanding secondary and higher education far beyond what had been done in the 1960s.

Enrollments in secondary education rose steadily, from 272,193 in 1970/71 to a high of 1,182,600 in 1981/82, dipped by almost 66,000 in 1982/83 and then rose again in 1983/84 (see Table 4.1). In 1970/71, only 63.8 percent of the thirteen-to-sixteen-year-old cohort was in school, while in 1981/82 this figure had risen to 84.0 percent.[43] Since secondary education still required expansion in the early 1980s, the reason for the 1982/83 drop in enrollment is unclear. In any event, the trend was for secondary education enrollments to expand dramatically after 1970.

From the limited data available, it would seem that, as the secondary system expanded, it also became more efficient. Retention rates, the ratio between the number of students enrolled at the beginning of a particular year and the number enrolled at the end of that academic year, increased for all types of secondary schools for which data are available (see Table 4.3).

Since the figures are obtained by dividing the number of students at the beginning of the school year by the number of students at the end of the year, it should be noted that retention bears no necessary relationship to the number of students who passed an academic year, for it includes those still enrolled at the end of the year whether they passed or failed. Moreover, retention rates give only a rough estimate of the numbers of students who dropped out of school during the school year, for these

Table 4.3

Percentage of Students' Retention in Various Types of Cuban Secondary Schools, 1970/71 and 1982/83

Type of School	Retention	
	1970/71	1982/83
Basic Secondary (Grades 7-9)	84.1%	94.2%
Preuniversity (Grades 10-12)	86.9	93.2
Polytechnical (Grades 7-13)	N.A.	87.7
Teacher Training (Grades 10-13)	72.8	92.5

Sources: For 1970/71, Ministerio de Educación, Informe a la Asamblea Nacional del Poder Popular (Havana: 1981), p. 252; for 1982/83, Ministerio de Educación, Organización de la educación 1981-1983, informe a la XXXIX Conferencia Internacional de Educación, Ginebra, Suiza 1984 (Havana: 1984), p. 177.

would be partly compensated for by those who entered school late in the academic year. But even with these limitations in mind, the improved retention rates suggest that the efficiency of Cuba's secondary education system increased substantially after 1970.

Although ignored in much of the literature on revolutionary Cuba, some of the more dramatic changes in Cuban education after 1970 took place at the higher education level. In 1974/75 the country still had only five centers of higher education, but by 1984/85 it had forty-six.[44] Enrollment at this level expanded from 35,137 in 1970/71 to 205,000 in 1980/81, stagnated for a couple of years, and then reached 240,000 in 1984/85 (see Table 4.1). Between 1970/71 and 1984/85, higher education enrollments increased by a remarkable 583 percent.

After 1970, the Cubans also began to develop a system of graduate education in their major university centers. Until the early 1970s, graduate education was limited to summer courses, designed for the professional improvement of the higher education teaching staff. These courses did not lead to advanced degrees, and were taught by foreign experts. By 1971, however, a system for granting advanced degrees at the masters and doctoral levels was being developed, and in 1972 a Commission for the Study of Scientific Grades was set up to determine the objectives and requirements for advanced degrees for professors, researchers, and new professionals in production and services.[45] In 1982/83 alone, almost 1,900 students were attending 994 graduate courses.[46]

Not only did higher education enrollments expand after 1970, but their distribution by subject area changed considerably (see Table 4.4). As the post–1970 development strategy placed less stress on agricultural and more on industrial expansion, technology enrollments outpaced those in agricultural sciences. Enrollments in humanities, social sciences, and art, economic studies, and education, which had all declined in absolute as well as relative numbers in the 1960s, expanded the most in the 1970s. The dramatic 4,725.6 percent increase in education enrollments signified the emphasis put on improving teachers' qualifications. The impressive 1,665.2 percent increase in economic studies enrollments went hand in hand with the replacement of the *fidelista* system by organizational structures that increased the demand for economic professionals after 1970.

In order to meet this increased demand, after 1970 education in economic studies was revamped. In the 1970/71 academic year, a new Institute of Economy was created at Camaguey to complement those that had already existed in the 1960s at Santiago, Santa Clara, and Havana.[47] In 1973/74, the then-Vice-ministry of Higher Education sought to overcome the results of the *fidelista* denigration of economic studies in the 1960s by creating a unified national curriculum for training economic professionals. Study toward the degree of Licentiate in Political Economy was begun in 1974/75, to train future professors for the new curriculum.[48]

In June 1970, the Institute of Economy at the University of Havana initiated its first graduate courses, aimed at upgrading and expanding the skills and knowledge of those who had been trained in the 1960s. In August 1973, the first masters degrees were granted to students in economic regional planning.[49] Beginning in 1973/74, it became possible for those in economic studies in Cuba to prepare for the degree of Candidato a Doctor en Ciencias Economicas, which would be granted by Moscow State University.[50] By 1982, seventeen Cuban professors had successfully completed this degree.[51]

A National School of Economic Management (Escuela Nacional de Dirección de la Economía—ENDE) was opened in 1976.[52] This was specifically created to train economic professionals in the workings of the new organizational structures gradually introduced in the economy in the late 1970s and early 1980s, discussed above. After the first semester of ENDE's existence, it became clear that diffusing this knowledge to all who needed it was too much for this one school. Beginning in July

Table 4.4
Cuban Higher Education Enrollments by Subject Area, 1969/70 and 1979/80

| Subject Area | Enrollment | | Percentage Change |
	1969/70	1979/80	1969/70 - 1979/80
Agricultural Sciences	5,154	19,628	280.8%
Technology	7,948	36,252	356.1
Natural and Exact Sciences	3,420	8,813	157.7
Medical Sciences	7,977	23,033	188.7
Humanities, Social Sciences, and Art	2,178	12,618	479.3
Education	1,627	78,513	4,725.6
Economic Studies	1,214	21,431	1,665.2
Total	29,518	200,288	578.5

Sources: For 1969/70, Ministerio de Educación Superior, Informe de la delegación de la Republica de Cuba a la VII Conferencia de Ministros de Educación Superior y Media Especializada de los Países Socialistas (Havana: 1972), pp. 117-118. For 1979/80, author's computations based on the total enrollment figures and the percent distribution of enrollment by "specialty" (Grupo de Especialidad) given in Ministerio de Educación, Informe a la Asamblea Nacional del Poder Popular (Havana: 1981), pp. 346, 365. All percentage change figures computed by author.

Note: The total enrollment figure for 1969/70 given in the first source above is somewhat lower than that given in the second and used in Table 3.1. The most likely reason for this discrepancy is that the first source may not include some categories of higher education enrollments, such as in correspondence courses. The first source is used here because only it breaks enrollment down by "Faculty," here labelled "Subject Area." Until 1977, Cuban higher education was organized according to "Faculties," and thereafter according to "Specialties." See "Ley que establice la estructura de especializaciones para la educación superior," Universidad de la Habana, Nos. 203/204 (1976), pp. 175-179. The second source provides no breakdown for 1969/70, and breaks 1979/80 enrollment down by "Specialty." In order to make the figures for the two years reported compatible, the author has had to judge which "Specialty" would have belonged to which "Faculty," if the latter were still the organizing principle in force; thus, there is some chance of error here, but probably not much.

1976, offshoots of ENDE were set up across the country, and by 1980 each province had such a school. Between 1976 and 1980, this network of schools trained 10,101 students, of which 5,608 were enterprise managers, 3,567, assistant economic managers, 627, state and organizational managers, and 290, professors.[53] In 1978, ENDE came under the direction of the Central Planning Agency (JUCEPLAN) and was changed into the Higher Institute of Economic Management. In 1985, this institute graduated its first cohort of Licentiates in Economic Management.

After 1970, as the supply of economic and other new professionals was increased through educational expansion and improvement, the educational system was also modified in the hope of producing new professionals with a revolutionary rather than an elitist or technocratic consciousness. The revolutionary leadership was aware that new professionals might attempt to parlay their knowledge and skill advantages into material privileges, and to arrogate to themselves, as experts, the right to make decisions bureaucratically without popular participation, ignoring the interests or expressed desires of the regime's popular base. Therefore, the revolutionary leadership called on the educational system to form new professionals who would also be New Persons committed to the principles of democratic centralism. To do this, after 1970 the principle of combining study with work (*estudio-trabajo*) was for the first time systematically introduced into Cuban education.[54] Although this principle was applied to all levels of the regular educational system, its most far-reaching application was at the secondary and higher education levels, responsible for training the new professionals.[55]

The practice of work-study goes back as far as 1962, when tens of thousands of secondary scholarship students were mobilized to harvest coffee in Oriente Province. Work-study was promulgated as a principle of Cuban education as early as 1964. Resolution 392 of that year called for educational programs that would combine "physical labor with intellectual work, and both of these with life."[56] From the early 1960s on, secondary school students were periodically mobilized to work in industry or agriculture on weekends, holidays, or when demand for labor was particularly high, as during the sugar harvest. In 1966, as the whole society mobilized to expand sugar production, the "school to the countryside" program was born. In this program, analogous to voluntary labor in the rest of the society, secondary students and their teachers travelled to the countryside to engage in various types of agricultural work for a period of thirty-five days a year.[57]

But, as the National Congress of Education and Culture found in 1971, these early efforts did not involve all secondary school students nor systematically combine work and study. Instead, these mobilizations were isolated events that frequently had a negative impact on education. They often interrupted the course of academic studies and hurt academic performance. In addition, they were too short to instill a New Person mentality. As a Cuban teacher later explained to me, for the students in these programs, "work and study remained separate, even contradictory, realms."[58]

Despite these criticisms, in 1972/73 the "school to the countryside" program was generalized to the whole regular secondary school system. Except for vocational and technical schools, where the curriculum already combined work with study, this was considered a transitional measure. For basic secondary and preuniversity schools—the training grounds for the bulk of the new professionals—the curriculum was more general and academic; there, the "school *to* the countryside" program would be replaced by "schools *in* the countryside."[59]

Students board at schools in the countryside during the week and return home on weekends. The school day is divided into two shifts, one for study and the other for agricultural work on the state farm on which the school is located. Students are organized into work brigades according to their year in school, and spend three hours of each school day doing agricultural work. Each school ordinarily houses above five hundred students who, along with a regular adult labor force, are responsible for a little over five hundred hectares of state farm land, usually devoted to tobacco, citrus fruits, or other foods. Each task performed by the student work brigades has output norms, set at about half the productivity rate of a normal adult worker.[60]

These schools attempt to instill in new professionals-in-training, during their formative teenage years, a producer's rather than a consumer's consciousness, to make them aware and appreciative of the work and skill that ordinary producers devote to every item of consumption. In addition, it is hoped that, by actually seeing their work bear fruit in an agricultural product, students will learn to value and find joy in work. Finally, these schools are designed to familiarize urban students with the agricultural basis of the country's heritage and society, and to instill in them a respect for the rural population and its critical role in Cuba's economic development. In short, schools in the countryside are supposed to form New Persons for Cuba.[61]

It is clear, of course, that schools in the countryside can achieve this goal only if they are attended by a sizable share of secondary students. Although the number of secondary-level schools in the countryside reached 556 by 1980/81,[62] development of these schools had begun to

Table 4.5
Number and Percentage of Students in Cuban Basic Secondary and Preuniversity "Schools in the Countryside," for Selected Years, 1971/72 to 1980/81

Type of School	Students			
	1971/72	1974/75	1977/78	1980/81
Basic Secondary: (Grades 7-9)	186,115	307,209	556,845	677,590
In the countryside	3,438	75,488	201,894	211,784
Percentage in the countryside	1.8%	24.6%	36.3%	31.3%
Preuniversity: (Grades 10-12)	15,695	30,315	88,743	159,671
In the countryside	0	9,594	41,688	71,760
Percentage in the countryside	0.0%	31.6%	47.0%	44.9%
Total:	201,810	337,524	645,588	837,261
In the countryside	3,438	85,082	243,582	283,544
Percentage in the countryside	1.7%	25.2%	37.7%	33.9%

Source: Ministerio de Educación, Informe a la Asamblea Nacional del Poder Popular (Havana: 1981), pp. 344-346; and author's computations.

fall behind the growth of the relevant secondary student population by the beginning of the 1980s (see Table 4.5). The percentage of basic secondary and preuniversity students in schools in the countryside rose to 37.7 in 1977/78, but then fell to 33.9 by 1980/81. In part, this was most likely the result of rapidly increasing school enrollments combined with the fact that schools in the countryside had proven more costly to build and maintain than initially projected.[63] But it might also have reflected some level of popular discontent with this program. I have spoken with a number of Cubans, some of whose children had recently entered schools in the countryside, who were critical of such schools. In 1980, one went so far as to suggest that boarding children in the countryside was "destroying the Cuban family."[64] My sense, however, was and remains that most Cubans support this program.

In the 1960s, work-study in higher education, as at the secondary level, failed to involve all students and to truly combine work and study.[65] Only after 1970 was the work-study principle applied systematically in higher education. On the one hand, greater numbers of correspondence and evening courses, and even university teaching units within work centers, were created for workers and administrative personnel with regular jobs who had completed their secondary education. In the 1960s, such students were relatively few, but by the 1979/80 academic year they numbered 110,988, or 54.4 percent of total higher education enrollments.[66] On the other hand, in 1971 Fidel Castro announced the first systematic program of work-study for regular higher education students. This new system incorporated four hours of work into each regular day of study, that is, Monday through Friday. Initially, students spent twenty hours a week at work, twenty in classes, and twenty in individual or collective study. Beginning in 1977/78, weekly study was increased to between thirty and thirty-six hours.[67]

This new system also underwent other changes in its first few years. At first, there was some controversy over whether students should be required to engage in base work (*trabajo de base*), that is, manual or physical work on the shop floor and in the fields, or in specialized work (*trabajo especializado*), that is, nonmanual work in their specialty. One empirical study came out very strongly in favor of base work; the authors claimed it best overcame the manual-mental distinction in the minds of students, who, without the experience, might begin to consider themselves "better" than workers.[68]

Although base work predominated in the first few years of the new system, it was soon replaced totally with specialized work. In 1975, the First Congress of the Communist Party of Cuba officially recognized this change as correct. Work at the higher education level was to be "related essentially to professional formation."[69] Doubtlessly base work was rejected because it came too close to the *modus operandi* of the widely criticized *fidelista* model that was then being jettisoned. Furthermore, base work was probably not as effective as specialized work for reinforcing the skills that students were supposed to acquire and for socializing them into their future role in the democratic centralist decision-making process. In an apparent attempt to help overcome the manual-mental distinction without resorting to base work, in 1973 the revolutionary leadership instituted a period of social service (*servicio social*) for all higher education graduates, requiring them to work in rural areas or in other Third World countries for a period of two to three years upon graduation.[70]

In whatever form, the new work-study system was rapidly implemented.[71] As early as the 1972/73 academic year, all but 5 percent of the students at the University of Havana, for example, were involved. Once a series of initial problems were ironed out, the new work-study system was reported to have beneficial results. The system was credited with having helped raise the level of discipline, political consciousness, and the promotion rate of the new professionals-in-training.[72]

As will become evident in Chapter 6, the performance of the organizational structures and motivating mechanisms introduced after 1970 has been marred by bureaucratic centralist practices. Of interest here, however, have been the aims behind the post–1970 rectification process, rather than its ultimate results. Through this process, the revolutionary leadership attempted to institutionalize a balanced incentive system, a differentiated organizational setup, and democratic centralist operating principles. By personally interlocking the Party with other organizational structures, the revolutionary leadership attempted to ensure that the societal decisions it reserved to itself would ultimately prevail. But the leadership also partially differentiated the Party from these other structures. This opened the way for mass participation, as a way of solidifying popular support. And it increased the demand for new professionals to competently operate the new semi-autonomous organizations. To meet this demand, and to form new professionals with a revolutionary and democratic centralist consciousness, the revolutionary leadership modified the educational system, as we have seen, with enormous implications for the size, makeup, and future of the new professionals.

NOTES

1. Although the post–1970 years are commonly characterized by both Cubans and Cuba scholars as a period of "institutionalization" of new organizations and procedures, this was only one aspect of the changes introduced. At the very least, this characterization ignores the change in development strategy and the dramatic expansion and transformation of education after 1970. It is, therefore, more accurate to characterize this period as one of "rectification," of which "institutionalization" formed only a part.

2. Author's computations based on the estimates of Claes Brundenius, *Revolutionary Cuba: The Challenge of Economic Growth with Equity* (Boulder, Colorado: Westview Press, 1984), p. 40.

3. Gonzalo M. Rodríguez Mesa, "El desarrollo industrial de Cuba y la

maduración de inversiones,'' *Economía y Desarrollo* 68 (May-June 1982), p. 127.

4. Max Weber, "Bureaucracy," in Hans Gerth and C. Wright Mills, eds., *From Max Weber: Essays in Sociology* (New York: Oxford University Press, 1958), pp. 196–244.

5. This term stems from the writings of Lenin and the subsequent interpretations of these writings in Soviet Marxism. In order to understand the significance of this term in contemporary Cuba, however, there is no need to trace this history. The Cubans have amply explained what they mean by "democratic centralist" process. See Orlando Carnota, "La profesión de administrador," *Economía y Desarrollo* 23 (May-June 1974), pp. 47–67; and Ovidio D'Angelo Hernández, "Algunos aspectos sociales de la gestión de empresas," *Economía y Desarrollo* 44 (Nov.-Dec. 1977), pp. 30–45.

6. Of course, the principles of democratic centralism are simply too general to answer all questions that may arise about the decision-making process. For example, to what extent do the higher levels set the agenda and predefine the problems to be discussed in the first step? Is it legitimate in the second step to assume, as the Cubans sometimes have, that decisions made by higher-level leaders will coincide with the general interest, as if leaders never have particularistic interests of their own? Under what conditions might higher-level leaders usurp the decision-making responsibilities of lower-level leaders in the second step? If final decisions are monopolized by the leadership levels, even if the rationales for these decisions are thoroughly explained, how willingly will lower levels actively cooperate in implementating and controlling these decisions in the third step? And if the lower levels drag their feet, can decisions be considered "optimal" in any practical sense?

7. *Granma Weekly Review*, May 7, 1972.

8. Alfredo Suarez, General Secretary, Transport Workers Union, as quoted in Marifeli Pérez-Stable, "Whither the Cuban Working Class?" *Latin American Perspectives*, Supplement 1975, p. 70.

9. Although Cuban workers were given no formal authority to fire managers, those interviewed by Linda Fuller in 1982 and 1983 "expressed confidence that they could have a decisive hand in the dismissal of an administrator" through their union. Fuller also found three cases—two in one workplace—where this had happened. See her "Politics of Workers' Control in Cuba 1959–1983: The Work Center and the National Arena" (Ph.D. diss., University of California, Berkeley, 1985), pp. 423–25; and "Changes in the Relationship among Unions, Administration, and the Party at the Cuban Workplace, 1959–1982," *Latin American Perspectives*, 13, 2 (Spring 1986), pp. 6–32.

10. *Memorias del XIII Congreso de la CTC* (Havana: 1973), pp. 15, 181. Among other things, this Congress also approved the institution of (1) monthly worker/management production and services assemblies, where all would discuss the basic production issues of the enterprise or work center; (2) collective work commitments, in which workers would formally commit themselves to meeting

the production plan, etc., and management would commit itself to protecting workers' safety, etc.; and (3) enterprise and work center management councils, on which a union representative would sit along with the manager, technical personnel, and a representative of the Party.

11. See Arthur MacEwan, "Incentives, Equality, and Power in Revolutionary Cuba," in Ronald Radosh, ed., *The New Cuba* (New York: Morrow, 1976), p. 89.

12. Author's interview HG01.80.

13. For these new scales, see Claes Brundenius, *Economic Growth, Basic Needs and Income Distribution in Revolutionary Cuba* (Lund, Sweden: University of Lund, 1981), p. 153; for an explanation of this reform and its official rationale, see "General Wage Reform," *Granma Weekly Review*, April 6, 1980, pp. 4–5; and Joaquín Benavides Rodríguez, "La ley de la distribución con arreglo al trabajo y la reforma de salarios en Cuba," *Cuba Socialista* 2 (Mar. 1982), pp. 62–93. According to information reported by Marifeli Pérez-Stable, "Politics and Conciencia in Revolutionary Cuba, 1959–1984" (Ph.D. diss., State University of New York at Stony Brook, 1985), p. 200, bonuses could now constitute 15 to 25 percent of an individual's salary.

14. Author's computation based on data supplied by Eugenio Balari, Director of the Cuban Institute of Internal Demand.

15. For a detailed discussion of the parallel market and the rationale behind it, see Humberto Pérez, *Sobre las dificultades objetivas de la revolución: lo que el pueblo deber saber* (Havana: Editorial Política, 1979), pp. 82–92.

16. For useful information on these changes, see "Cuba's New 'Free Market,' " *Cuba Update*, 1, 3 (Sept. 1980), pp. 1–2; and Medea Benjamin et al., *No Free Lunch: Food and Revolution in Cuba Today* (San Francisco: Institute for Food and Development Policy, 1984), chap. 5.

17. See the text of this law in *Revista Cubana de Derecho* 24 (1985), pp. 37–78.

18. Useful information on the structure and operation of the SDPE can be found in almost every issue of *Economía y Desarrollo* since the mid–1970s, and in "Sobre el sistema de dirección y planificación de la economía," in Primer Congreso del Partido Communista de Cuba, *Tesis y resoluciones* (Havana: Editorial de Ciéncias Sociales, 1978), pp. 189–207; Raúl Martel, *La empresa socialista* (Havana: Editorial de Ciéncias Sociales, 1979); Enrique Corona Zayas, *Los contratos económicos y el arbitraje en la legislación de SDPE* (Havana: Centro de Información Científico Técnica de JUCEPLAN, 1979); *Sistema de arbitraje estatal y normas básicas para los contratos económicos* (Havana: Editorial Obre, 1978); *Segunda plenaria nacional de chequeo de la implantación del SDPE* (Havana: Ediciones JUCEPLAN, 1980); Fuller, *Politics*, chap. 7.

19. Nine percent of Cuban enterprises were under SDPE by 1978, 55.8 percent by 1979, and 94.8 percent by 1980, according to Justa Hernández Hernández and Vasili Nikolenkov, "El mecanismo económico del socialismo," *Economía y Desarrollo* 68 (Sept.-Oct. 1985), p. 77. It is important to note that these figures apply to enterprises, not work centers, which are local subunits of enterprises.

20. Osvaldo Dorticós, *Discurso en el acto de presentación de los militantes del partido del Instituto de Economía* (Havana: Editorial de Ciéncias Sociales, 1969).

21. Osvaldo Dorticós, "Control económico y normación: tareas del primer orden," *Economía y Desarrollo* 11 (May-June 1972), p. 34.

22. Until 1984, these would have been the officials of the *Junta Central de Planificación* (JUCEPLAN), but, in late 1984, JUCEPLAN was considerably weakened and many of its functions were taken over by the *Grupo Estatal Central* (Central Group), made up of members of the Executive Committee of the Council of Ministers. This change took place, according to Fidel Castro, because JUCEPLAN had too easily given in to the demands of the various ministries, and had failed to limit and coordinate these demands in the interest of the economy as a whole. On this, see *Granma Weekly Review*, Dec. 29, 1984; Jan. 4, 1985; and Feb. 11, 1985.

23. Although workers were to exercise no control over the national economic plan, they were supposed to influence the role of their enterprise and work center in that plan. For a description of the planning process at the work center level, see Marta Harneker, *Cuba: Dictatorship or Democracy?* (Westport, CN: Lawrence Hill, 1980), chap. 1.

24. SDPE initially envisioned a third incentive fund to finance microinvestments by the enterprise, but this has apparently not been instituted in Cuba.

25. The details on the formal structure of the OPP are taken from the *Constitution of the Republic of Cuba* (New York: Center for Cuban Studies, 1976), chaps. 7–9; *Reglamento de las Asambleas Nacional, Provincial, y Municipal del Poder Popular* (Havana: Editorial Obre, 1979); Carollee Bengelsdorf, "A Large School of Government," *Cuba Review*, 6, 3 (Sept. 1976), pp. 3–18, and "Between Visions and Reality: Democracy in Socialist Theory and Practice" (Ph.D. diss., Massachusetts Institute of Technology, 1985); Lourdes Casal, "On Popular Power: The Organization of the Cuban State during the Period of Transition," *Latin American Perspectives*, Supplement 1975, pp. 78–88; Cynthia Cockburn, "People's Power," in John Griffiths and Peter Griffiths, eds., *Cuba: The Second Decade* (London: Writers and Readers Publishing Cooperative, 1979), pp. 18–35; Archibald R. M. Ritter, "The Organs of People's Power and the Communist Party: The Nature of Cuban Democracy," in Sandor Halebsky and John M. Kirk, eds., *Cuba: Twenty-Five Years of Revolution* (New York: Praeger, 1985), pp. 270–90; and Harnecker, *Cuba*.

26. According to Andrew Zimbalist, the municipal OPPs oversee about 34 percent of the production and service units. See his "Cuban Economic Planning: Organization and Performance," p. 223, in Halebsky and Kirk, *Cuba*.

27. *Cuban Constitution*, Chap. 7, Art. 68. By creating this assembly, however, the Cubans have not jettisoned their normal practice of widely discussing drafts of fundamental laws and other important political documents with the population. As the Constitution stipulates, "when it is considered necessary in view of the nature of the law in question," the National OPP Assembly may "submit it to the people for consultation," Chap. 7, Art. 73.

28. For a brief discussion of the Cuban electoral and nominating system, see René González Mendoza, "The Electoral System in Cuba," *Granma Weekly Review*, Dec. 21, 1986, p. 2.

29. Fifty-five percent of the delegates to the National OPP Assembly must have been elected at the municipal level.

30. See, for example, Cockburn, "People's Power," p. 27; and Ritter, "The Organs of People's Power," p. 279. In 1979, according to Ritter's figures, Communist Party and Union of Young Communist members predominated for the first time at the municipal level as well. Although the reasons for this are unclear, a Young Communist told me in 1980 that others had become reluctant to accept OPP positions because of the time and energy involved. Author's interview CMS.80.

31. In Michael Taber, ed., *Fidel Castro Speeches, Vol. 2: Our Power Is that of the Working People*. (New York: Pathfinder Press, 1983), pp. 234–35.

32. Although they cannot be discussed in detail here, since 1970 the Party has undergone a series of other changes as well. Perhaps most important, it has held regular congresses, developed an explicit program, and expanded its membership considerably.

33. See "Sobre la política de formación, selección, ubicación, promoción y superación de los cuadros," in Primer Congreso, pp. 57–99.

34. Ministerio de Educación, *El plan de perfeccionamiento y desarrollo del Sistema Nacional de Educación de Cuba* (Havana: 1976), p. 11.

35. Ministerio de Educación, *El plan de perfeccionamiento*, "Introducción"; and Primer Congreso, pp. 363–422.

36. The 1980 figure was reported by Brundenius, *Economic Growth*, p. 125. The 1981 figure is from *Granma Weekly Review*, Jan. 29, 1984, p. 4.

37. Fidel Castro, "Main Report to the Third Congress of the Communist Party of Cuba," *Granma Weekly Review*, Feb. 16, 1986, p. 5.

38. Sergio Díaz-Briquets and Lisandro Pérez, *Cuba: The Demography of Revolution* (Washington, D.C.: The Population Reference Bureau, 1981), pp. 12–13.

39. For 1974/75, Ministerio de Educación, *Informe a la Asamblea Nacional del Poder Popular* (Havana: 1981), p. 372; for 1980/81, *Granma Weekly Review*, Jan. 29, 1984, p. 4.

40. Ministerio de Educación, *El plan de perfeccionamiento*, p. 63.

41. Nikolai Kolesnikov, *Cuba: educación popular y preparación de los cuadros nacionales, 1959–1982* (Moscow: Editorial Progreso, 1983), p. 287. The Cubans attribute these advances to a variety of post–1970 curricular and other changes and to improved teacher training, neither of which can be discussed here. See "Interview with José R. Fernández, Minister of Education," and "Teaching Staff Improvements," *Cuba Update*, 1, 6 (Jan. 1981), pp. 3 and 12, respectively.

42. See "Ley que crea el Ministerio de Educación Superior," *Universidad de la Habana*, Nos. 203/204 (1976), pp. 171–175.

43. For 1970/71, Ministerio de Educación, *Informe*, p. 372; for 1981/82, Kolesnikov, *Cuba*, p. 285.

44. For 1974/75, Concepción Duchesne, "Incremento y desarrollo en la educación superior, 1976–1980," *Bohemia*, Nov. 28, 1980, p. 36; for 1984/85, Fidel Castro, "Main Report to the Third Congress," p. 5.

45. *Economía y Desarrollo* 14 (Nov.-Dec. 1972), p. 212.

46. Kolesnikov, *Cuba*, p. 422. For further details on the Cuban system of graduate education, see Emilio Fernández Conde, "La educación postgraduada," *Sobre Educación Superior*, July–Dec. 1971, pp. 77–92; the summary of the report of the Cuban delegation to the Sixth Conference of Ministers of Higher Education of the Socialist Countries, in Bucharest, October 1971, in *Economía y Desarrollo* 9 (Jan.-Feb. 1972), esp., pp. 212–14; Oscar F. Rego, "Los cursos de postgrado especializados," *Bohemia*, Nov. 30, 1979; and Concepción Duchesne, "Superación professional," *Bohemia*, Jan. 23, 1981.

47. "Academicas," *Economía y Desarrollo* 13 (Sept.-Oct. 1972), p. 225.

48. Alexis Codina Jimínez and Joaquín Fernández, "Apuntos en el XX aniversario del inicio de la formación de economistas," *Economiía y Desarrollo* 71 (Nov.-Dec. 1982), pp. 23–25.

49. *Economía y Desarrollo* 18 (July-Aug. 1973), p. 210.

50. "Academicas," *Economía y Desarrollo* 23 (May-June 1974).

51. Codina Jiménez and Fernández, "Apuntos en el XX aniversario," p. 32.

52. Rosendo Morales, "La preparación de los cuadros dirigentes de la economía del pais," *Cuba Socialista* 4 (Nov.-Dec. 1982), pp. 108–33.

53. Ibid., pp. 119–20.

54. Besides this hoped for political benefit, the Cubans introduced work-study also for material and practical reasons. To make secondary and even higher education universally available to the population is a stated goal of the revolution. Such an accomplishment would strain the resources of most societies, and would normally be beyond the reach of relatively poor countries like Cuba. By having those who study also work, however, the Cubans hope to generate a substantial proportion of the resources expended on the maintenance and expansion of the educational system.

55. At the primary level, the work-study principle has been applied in the form of student-tended school gardens and students' helping to clean and care for their school. See Karen Wald, *Children of Che* (Palo Alto, CA: Ramparts Press, 1978), p. 180.

56. Quoted in Max Figueroa et al., *The Basic Secondary School in the Countryside: An Educational Innovation in Cuba* (Paris: UNESCO, 1974), p. 11. As the Cubans point out, their ideas concerning the combination of work and study have their origins in the writings of Karl Marx and José Martí, the Cuban revolutionary leader of the late nineteenth century. Marx, of course, emphasized the need to overcome the social and psychological separation of manual and mental work in order to create an egalitarian society composed of fully developed human beings. Martí put forth similar ideas, often couched in poetic prose: "In

countries such as ours there must be a thorough-going revolution in education if we do not wish to see them—as some are already—perpetually distorted, wasted, and deformed, like the Horatian monster—with a gigantic head and an immense heart, trailing its flagging feet, its withered arms all skin and bones.'' Quoted in Figueroa, p. 9.

57. For this historical background, see Figueroa, pp. 10–12; and UNCTAD, *Health and Education Technology in Cuba* (New York: United Nations Organization, 1979), pp. 22–23.

58. Author's interview ST2.80.

59. Marvin Leiner seems to assume that it is Cuban policy to extend the school in the countryside program to all of secondary education, including technical and vocational schools. He calls the development of special technical and vocational schools at the upper secondary level an "exception" to the use of the school in the countryside program as a mechanism for creating the New Person. These special schools select the best students, as measured by national competitive examinations, for training in the natural sciences and certain technical vocations. Leiner reports that, although these schools use the same textbooks as other schools at their level, they offer superior teaching and equipment. In 1969, only one such school existed, but by the early 1980s each of the island's provinces possessed one of these schools. According to Fidel Castro, in 1984 these special schools served 24,000 students, a figure that would shortly expand to 26,000.

Leiner suggests that these schools introduced an element of elitism in Cuban secondary education. Castro, on the other hand, claims that these schools are necessary to help students in these more exacting subject areas to make a successful transition to even more demanding higher education. If Leiner is correct, the elitism introduced by these schools stems from the better quality of education they offer, not from the fact that students in these schools do not participate in the school in the countryside program that was always intended for basic secondary and preuniversity students, not for technical and vocational students. See Marvin Leiner, "Cuba's Schools: 25 Years Later," in Halebsky and Kirk, p. 38; and Fidel Castro, *We Were Born to Overcome, Not to Be Overrun* (Havana: Editorial Política, 1984), pp. 15–17.

60. Figueroa, *Basic Secondary School*, pp. 28, 41.

61. For these and other goals of these schools, see ibid., pp. 14–26.

62. Ministerio de Educación, *Informe*, p. 368.

63. CEPAL, *Cuba: estilo de desarrollo y políticos sociales* (Cerro del Agua, México: Siglo Veintiuno Editores, 1980), p. 97.

64. Author's interviews ST1.80, ST2.80, SHW1.80, SHW2.80, SMT.80, SP.80, and SOU.80.

65. For an overview of work-study in higher education in the 1960s, see Ministerio de Educación, *El principio de la combinación del trabajo en la educación superior: Informe a la conferencia de ministros de educación superior de países socialistas* (Havana: 1974), pp. 26–35.

66. Duchesne, "Superación professional," p. 35.

67. Ministerio de Educación, *El principio*, p. 39; and Kolesnikov, *Cuba*, p. 191.

68. Niurka Pérez and Elena Díaz, "Primera experiencia de inserción laboral en la facultad de ciéncias: estudio exploratoria," *Sobre Educación Superior*, Jan.–June 1975, pp. 60–62.

69. Primer Congreso, p. 386.

70. For information on this social service requirement, see Luís Rodríguez Balmaseda, "El servicio social: una positiva experiencia en la vida graduado," *Bohemia*, Aug. 13, 1982; and "Dictan regulaciones sobre facilidades para graduados que cumplen el servicio social," *Trabajadores*, Aug. 13, 1985.

71. Ministerio de Educación, *El principio*, pp. 39–42.

72. Ministerio de Educación, *El principio*, pp. 49–50; and Elena Pérez and Niurka Pérez, "Estudio sobre la integración estudiantil a los centros trabajo," *Sobre Educación Superior*, Jan.–June 1975, pp. 77–92.

5

Managing the Transition: From Old Cadres to New Professionals

Because some lose, some gain, some must reform themselves, and everyone must adjust, extensive sociopolitical changes never take place automatically. The post–1970 rectification process in Cuba has been no exception. On the one hand, it set the decline of the old cadres, who had risen in the 1960s to intermediate-level positions on the basis of political credentials. In the short run, some old cadres might resist this decline. But over the long run, they would all either lose their positions or convert themselves into new professionals through further education. On the other hand, the post–1970 rectification process both demanded and supplied an increasing number of new professionals to enter intermediate positions on the basis of educational credentials. If the new system were to operate according to design, revolutionary leaders would have to share some decision making with new professionals. And new professionals would have to develop a revolutionary consciousness.

How has the revolutionary leadership attempted to manage this transition, and how has it progressed? How has the leadership dealt with the old cadres who have occupied intermediate-level positions? At what point did the number of new professionals catch up with the drain of skilled personnel leaving the country? From what social origins have these new professionals arisen? And how has the revolutionary leadership attempted to define concretely their decision-making role? These are some of the major questions to which we now turn.

CRITICIZING AND REASSURING THE OLD CADRES

The old cadres have been often criticized for lacking the requisite experience, formal education, and know-how to perform their work well. In 1970, Fidel Castro himself used this administrative inadequacy to help explain the failure to reach that year's 10-million-ton sugar goal. After that, public complaints of this sort by leaders and new professionals became commonplace.

The basis of such criticisms is evident from the simple level of some of the how-to guides for administrators, written by new professionals for old cadres in the early 1970s. These typically contain very elementary guidelines—for using personal calendars, preparing reports and memos, using work plans, evaluating subordinates, and holding meetings. The following outline for carrying on a meeting is characteristic of this genre:

1. Be sure the meeting is necessary.
2. Invite only those who can add something to the discussion.
3. Use meetings only for collective discussion, not for disseminating information.
4. Conduct the meeting in an orderly fashion.
5. Attend to what is said.
6. Keep the discussion on the topic.
7. Stop when the topic is exhausted.
8. Achieve a concrete conclusion to the discussion.[1]

This list clearly illustrates the perception that many old cadres lack even the most basic administrative sense.

Old cadres have also been frequently criticized for being either "chatterers" or "super-executives." The first cover up their lack of knowledge or ability for organizing themselves and others to accomplish tasks by their constant incantation of revolutionary slogans, such as "Patria o Muerte!"[2] They spend the workday pretending to be busy by holding endless meetings, which are social gatherings rather than working sessions. Whether their chatter is revolutionary or social, they accomplish little and prevent others from accomplishing much.[3] Old cadre super-executives, on the other hand, prefer to work without a plan and are unable to delegate responsibility to subordinates. They rush from place to place, hop out of their jeep to check on the execution of other's tasks and issue orders, and then roar off again. They thrive on impressing others with their initiative, audacity, decisiveness, and dynamism, regardless of their concrete accomplishments, which are few.[4]

Both types of behavior can be seen as part of the legacy of the *fidelista* system of the late 1960s. Many chatterers and super-executives could be expected among cadres with little know-how, who were confronted with very ambitious goals and forced out of their offices into factories and fields by the anti-bureaucratic struggle. Many probably had little choice but to chatter or dash about. Criticisms of chatterers and super-executives began to be widely expressed publicly only in the first half of the 1970s; complaints about lack of skills and unsystematic work can still be heard in Cuba, indicating perhaps the persistence of this part of the *fidelista* legacy.[5]

Another aspect of this legacy has been no less enduring. In the *fidelista* period, it will be remembered, mass participation in decision making atrophied. The people lacked institutionalized means for making suggestions and registering complaints, and were expected simply to follow the orders of their superiors. Through this experience, many old cadres developed the habit of avoiding popular participation, and this seems to have lived on. As head of the Central Planning Agency (JUCEPLAN) at the end of the 1970s, Humberto Pérez stated: "The *compañeros* who work in the distinct state organizations, including those who work in those of Poder Popular, are impregnated with the old centralizing and in many cases bureaucratic habits."[6] Although some old cadres who remained in intermediate occupations after 1970 apparently overcame their bureaucratic habits, others did not.[7] As will be seen in the next chapter, the latter have been an important force blocking full implementation of democratic centralist principles.

The old cadres are destined for conversion into or replacement by new professionals. But, while many old cadres find self-transformation beyond their ability or inclination, they would like to prevent their own displacement. These old cadres have developed self-protective strategies for retaining intermediate-level positions despite their relative lack of formal training. Raúl Castro referred to them in October 1979 when he complained of individuals who "are more concerned about retaining the positions they hold then about the needs of the people they are supposed to serve."[8] He went on to explain that such administrative personnel typically engage in "buddyism," that is, they collude with coworkers to cover up poor work performance to protect their positions.[9] Buddyism is not solely a form of old cadre self-protection; new professionals may also sometimes engage in this behavior. But, given that old cadre positions are threatened in ways that new professional positions are not, buddyism is more likely to be characteristic of old cadres.

The revolutionary leadership has explicitly recognized and attempted to mitigate this problem of old cadre resistance. In 1975, it promulgated a policy for training, selecting, evaluating, improving, and promoting members of the administrative apparatus, designed in part to reassure old cadres.[10] This policy stipulates that everyone should be periodically and systematically evaluated in an objective rather than an arbitrary fashion, in order to prevent the development of "insecurity among the cadres."[11] According to this policy, objectivity can be guaranteed in two ways. First, it requires that personal traits not be the main focus except as they affect work performance, that everyone be allowed to appeal all evaluations, and that a wide range of people be consulted about each individual. Not only is the individual's immediate supervisor to be involved, but also coworkers, subordinates, trade union and Party officials, and others as well. Second, objective evaluations require that both positive and negative aspects of each individual's work performance be examined. The evaluation should not discourage but spur the individual to do better. Thus, the experience of the old cadres should be respected, and they should be encouraged to improve themselves through formal study. In other words, old cadres should be encouraged to convert themselves into new professionals. This, in part, explains the continuing viability of the adult education system, discussed earlier.

On the other hand, however, this policy stipulates that positions in the administrative apparatus should be awarded to those with the best formal educational preparation, and thereby favors the new professionals. But, as revolutionary leaders have admitted, they have faced difficulties in implementing this part of the policy. As will be noted in Chapter 7, old cadre administrators have often hired and promoted their old cadre "buddies" over their new professional competitors.[12] As late as 1988, Fidel Castro found it necessary to reiterate that intermediate-level positions must be awarded on the basis of educational credentials, not seniority, which, of course, favors the old cadres.[13]

Thus, the revolutionary leadership has been critical of old cadre work styles, incompetence, buddyism, and promotion by seniority. But, although it has favored the rise of the new professionals, it has recognized that the old cadres cannot be dispensed with overnight. It has been aware that, until the supply of new professionals was sufficiently large, old cadres might only be replaced by others with similar educational deficits and perhaps even less experience. So the leadership has opted, not for a rapid purge, but for a gradual transition. The revolutionary leadership

Table 5.1
Graduates of Secondary Schools in Cuba, 1959/60 through 1979/80

Year	Secondary School Graduates
1959/60 through 1961/62	17,583
1962/63 through 1964/65	14,324
1965/66 through 1967/68	23,810
1968/69 through 1970/71	28,495
1971/72 through 1973/74	35,269
1974/75 through 1976/77	125,827
1977/78 through 1979/80	265,649
Total	510,957

Source: Author's computations based on Ministerio de
    Educación, Informe a la Asamblea Nacional del Poder
    Popular (Havana: 1981), pp. 421-425, 427.

Note: These include all graduates of preuniversities,
    of polytechnical institutes at the medium-level
    technician grade, of secondary teacher education
    schools, and of secondary-level adult education
    schools, as well as graduates of medium-level
    technician courses offered by organizations other
    than the Ministry of Education.

has tried a policy that seeks to increase the chances that old cadres will convert themselves into new professionals and to reduce the possibility that old cadres will fear, and consequently resist, displacement by new professionals. But such resistance has occurred.

THE PACE OF THE TRANSITION AND THE SOCIAL ORIGINS OF THE NEW PROFESSIONALS

Whatever the level of resistance that some old cadres have mustered, however, the transition to the new professionals is destined to proceed. The pace of this transition can be seen partly in the results of Cuba's educational expansion (see Table 5.1). Between 1959/60 and 1979/80, 510,957 students gained the secondary degree that would allow them to enter intermediate-level occupations as new professionals. These data

Table 5.2
Estimated Change in Number of Cuban Refugee and Non-Refugee Secondary School Graduates, 1959–1980

	As of 1959	1959-1962	1963-1965	1966-1968	1969-1971	1972-1974	1975-1977	1978-1980
New Secondary School Graduates in Cuba	----	17,583	14,324	23,810	28,495	35,269	125,827	265,649
Refugee Labor Force Participants with Twelve or More Years of Schooling	----	31,519	9,512	21,010	18,466	2,942	1,398	10,505
Cumulative Total of Secondary School Graduates Remaining in Cuba	117,375	103,439	108,251	111,051	121,080	153,407	277,836	532,980

Sources: Top Line from Table 5.1.

Second line estimated and computed by author from figures for refugee labor force participants in Table 2.2 and various estimates of how many of these had 12 or more years of schooling. For 1959 through 1965, an estimate of 36.0 percent was used, based on Richard Fagan, et al., Cubans in Exile: Disaffection and Revolution (Stanford: Stanford University Press, 1968), p. 19; for 1965 through 1971, an estimate of 37.0 percent was used, based on the 1968 study by Eleanor Rogg, The Assimilation of Cuban Exiles (New York: Aberdeen Press, 1974), as cited in Alejandro Portes, et al., "The New Wave: A Statistical Profile of Recent Cuban Exiles to the United States," Cuban Studies/Estudios Cubanos, 7, 1 (Jan. 1977), p. 13; for 1972 through 1980, an estimate of 22.0 percent was used, based on data for 1973-1974 reported in Robert L. Bach, "The New Cuban Immigrants: Their Background and Prospects," in U.S. House of Representative, Committee on the Judiciary, Caribbean Migration, Ninety-Sixth Congress: 1980, p. 312.

Third line estimated and computed by author. The 117,375 figure for 1959 is the author's estimate based on 1953 Census figure of 99,143, increased by 18.39 percent, the same percentage increase as the total population over this period. The rest of these figures computed by subtracting the second line from the top line and adding the result to the previous total for this third line.

Note: Since data for the number of refugee secondary school graduates are not available, it was necessary to use the closest approximation, "twelve or more years of schooling." The category of Refugee Labor Force Participants with Twelve or More Years of Schooling includes some individuals without secondary diplomas, since prior to the 1977/78 academic year, Cuban students had to complete thirteen, not twelve, years of schooling to receive a secondary degree. See Ministerio de Educación, Documentos directivas para el perfeccionamiento del Sistema Nacional de Educación (Cuba: 1975), p. 35. Using the figures in this refugee category to compute the Cumulative Total of Secondary School Graduates Remaining in Cuba thus underestimates the number of secondary school graduates, the new professionals, left in the country. This underestimation is offset to some extent by two other factors that tend to overestimate the number of new professionals remaining in Cuba: First, these educational data do not make it possible to distinguish between new professionals and revolutionary leaders with comparable education. Second, no deduction for retirement and death has been made from these figures.

The alert reader will notice that using these educational data results in different estimates of the number of intermediate-level refugees in various years than did the occupational data used in Table 2.2. For 1959-62, the educational data result in a lower estimate, probably because in prerevolutionary Cuba some incumbents of intermediate occupations possessed fewer than twelve years of schooling. For all other years, and in total, the educational data result in higher estimates. There are probably two reasons for this: First, as explained above, since 13 years of schooling were needed to graduate before 1977/78, the number of refugee secondary school graduates is lower than the number with only 12 years of schooling. Second, some individuals probably left the country after completing twelve or more years of schooling but before entering the labor force at the intermediate-level.

There is no way to combine occupational and educational data to arrive at a uniform estimate of intermediate-level refugee labor force participants. Therefore, since both types of data are useful for different purposes, and since the estimates derived from these two types of data do not differ inordinately, it seems better to present both.

also illustrate the increasing pace at which new professionals have been supplied through educational expansion after 1970, and the extent to which Cuba's professionals are truly new. Just over one-half of the professionals educated between 1959 and 1980 in Cuba received their secondary school degrees since 1977, and well over four-fifths since 1971.

But when did the expansion of education begin to catch up with the drain of professionals through their exodus from Cuba? Estimating this requires adjusting for the number of intermediate-level personnel trained before the revolution, a considerable majority of whom, as seen in Chapter 2, did not leave the island. The expansion of Cuban secondary education after the revolution did not begin to match the exodus drain until the 1969–1971 period (see Table 5.2). The number of secondary school graduates remaining in Cuba dropped from an estimated 117,375 in 1959 to a low of 103,439 in the period 1959–1962. Even in the 1969–1971 period the 1959 figure was barely matched by the estimated 121,080 secondary school graduates remaining on the island. But during the 1970s, the number of secondary school graduates far outstripped the drain created by the exodus. By 1980, there were an estimated 532,980 secondary school graduates in Cuba, over four and one-half times as many as in 1959.[14]

This estimate of 532,980 secondary school graduates by 1980 can be combined with other data to roughly estimate three other figures. First, the total number of Cuban professionals with higher education degrees can be calculated for 1979 as 147,150.[15] This figure can be divided by 532,980 to estimate that roughly 28 percent of Cuban professionals held such higher degrees by 1980.

Second, some proportion of the 532,980 secondary school graduates in 1980 were pursuing their higher education full time, and were not actually in the labor force. Let us assume that these numbered 100,000, or slightly less than half of the total number of students—the rest being either part-time or correspondence students—enrolled in higher education in 1979/80 (see Table 4.1). Then, as estimated 432,980 new professionals were actually in the Cuban labor force in 1980.

Third, since the total number of Cubans in intermediate-level occupations was about 844,300 in 1979, the 432,980 new professionals in the labor force can be subtracted from this figure to estimate the number of old cadres at approximately 411,320.[16] According to this, by 1980 the new professionals had taken over roughly 51 percent of Cuba's intermediate-level positions, but the old cadres still held on to about 49 percent. These figures clearly illustrate the rise of the new professionals. But the fact that almost half of the intermediate-level posts by 1980 were still

Table 5.3
Percentage of New Entrants to the University of Havana by Highest
Educational Level of Parents, 1970/71

Highest Educational Level	Parents	
	Mother	Father
Not Specified	6%	8%
Primary (Grades 1-4)	60	49
Basic Secondary (Grades 5-9)	17	19
Advanced Secondary (Grades 10-13)	12	14
Higher Education	5	10
Total	100%	100%

Source: Ministerio de Educación, Informe de la delegación de la Republica de Cuba a la VII Conferencia
de Ministros de Educación Superior y Media
Especializada de los Países Socialistas (Havana:
1972), p. 52.

filled by old cadres is perhaps a result both if the revolutionary leadership's
policy of gradual transition from old cadres to new professionals and of
the old cadres' ability to resist displacement by new professionals.

From what social backgrounds have the new professionals come? Unfortunately, lack of data makes it impossible to answer this question with
assurance. But if the available information is manipulated with ingenuity,
it does suggest some interesting hypotheses.

The only available data concerns the educational levels of parents of
entrants to a single Cuban institution of higher education for one particular
year (see Table 5.3). Almost half of the new entrants to the University
of Havana in 1970/71 had fathers with only some primary schooling, and
60 percent had mothers with only such education. Furthermore, 19 percent
had fathers and 17 percent had mothers with only some basic secondary
training, while 14 percent had fathers and 12 percent mothers with some
advanced secondary education, and only 10 percent had fathers and 5
percent mothers with at least some higher education. The fact that the
parents of up to three-quarters of new entrants to the University of Havana
in 1970/71 had no more than a basic secondary education, of course,
suggests a dramatic redistribution of educational opportunities in the first
decade of the revolution.

Table 5.4
Estimated Chance of Potential Cuban Fathers of 1953 with Various Educational Backgrounds to Have Generated a Child Enrolled in Higher Education in 1970/71

Father's Educational Background	Potential Fathers, 1953 [a]	Higher Educ. Students, 1970/71	Chance of Pot. Fathers to have a Child in Higher Educ.
No Formal Education	321,736		
Not Specified		2,811	0.87%
Primary, (Grades 1-4)	923,132	17,217	1.87
Basic Secondary, (Grades 5-9)	39,431	6,676	16.93
Advanced Secondary, (Grades 10-13)	24,682	4,919	19.93
Higher Education	27,067	3,514	12.98
Total	1,336,048	35,137	2.63

Sources: "Potential fathers": author's computations based on the 1953 Censo de población. "Higher education students": author's computations from estimates based on the assumption that the distribution of father's education for all students in higher education in 1970/71, as given in Ministerio de Educación, Informe a la Asamblea Nacional del Poder Popular (1981), p. 345, was the same as for "new entrants to the University of Havana," as given in Table 5.3. Percentages in the third column: author's computations.

a. Males aged 15-44.

Assuming that these data were characteristic of all Cuban higher education students in that year, the chance of potential fathers, males aged 15–44 in 1953, to generate a child in higher education in 1970/71 can be estimated (see Table 5.4). Potential fathers as a whole had a 2.63 chance out of 100 to have such a child, while potential fathers with only primary education had less than 2 chances out of 100 to have such a child, and potential fathers with no formal education may have had less than 1 chance in a 100.[17] On the other hand, potential fathers with basic secondary and medium secondary educations had 17 and 20 chances out of 100, respectively, while those with higher education backgrounds had only 13 chances out of 100.[18]

In sum, these data suggest two hypotheses. On the one hand, after the first decade of the revolutionary process, children from prerevolutionary intermediate- and higher-level educational backgrounds still retained a relative advantage over those from lower-level backgrounds in their ability to enter higher education and to become new professionals. On the other hand, after the first decade of the revolution, children from prerevolutionary intermediate- and higher-level educational backgrounds had lost their nearly monopolistic advantage over those from lower-level backgrounds in this regard. There are no available data with which to trace this redistribution of educational chances beyond the revolution's first decade. Because of the character of the available data, it can only be suggested as an hypothesis that, by 1970/71, the majority of new professionals were originating from the upper levels of the lower, less educated stratum of Cuban society.

FAVORING THE NEW PROFESSIONALS AND DELIMITING THEIR ROLE

In a variety of ways already noted, the revolutionary leadership has favored the new professionals since 1970. First, the revolutionary leadership initiated the post–1970 rectification drive that increased both the demand for and supply of new professionals. Second, the revolutionary leadership promulgated the democratic centralist principles that, while justifying the subordination of the new professionals to the leadership, also justified for the former a clear and stable intermediate-level role within the rectified organizational setup. Third, the revolutionary leadership has favored the new professionals by giving them preference in intermediate-level employment, and by remunerating them in accordance with their education through the General Wage Reform of 1980.

But while favoring the new professionals, the revolutionary leadership has sought to clearly delimit their role. As already seen, through systematically introducing the principle of work-study in the educational system after 1970, the leadership attempted to instill a revolutionary consciousness in students, especially in those being prepared for intermediate-level posts. Even with this, however, there is an ever-present danger that new professionals will attempt to parlay their relative educational advantages into short- or long-term material privileges. Two Cuban economic studies students whom I interviewed expressed resentment over the fact that, as the supply of economic professionals rose, their official entry-level wages would fall. Although neither suggested that professionals should be able to corporately control their labor market, they considered it unfair that the students who were graduated before them had entered the market at higher wages than they could expect.[19] This points up the fact that, unlike the most developed professional groups in capitalist societies, Cuba's new professionals cannot control their labor market and wages.

But some of the new professionals have sought material privileges by other means. Speaking before the Union of Young Communists of 1982, Fidel Castro offered a striking example:

Mention was made at this congress of the lust for gain, and I think it is important to do so. I mean the lust for gain on the part of some professionals; certain highly telling examples were given, like the case of an engineer, an architect, or whatever, trained by the revolution, privately practicing his profession and charging exorbitant fees for drawing up simple plans for home repairs. . . . An ad in *Opina* . . . said: "Home repairs drawn up." A citizen comes to City Hall and is asked to present a plan for home repairs. An urbanization office, or what have you, asked for a little plan. The man charges 800, 900, 1,000 pesos for drawing up a little plan. . . . That's robbery being committed by a technician trained by the revolution.[20]

This particular abuse was curbed by having the Municipal Organs of Popular Power draw up such plans,[21] but the general problem remained. In 1986, Castro berated the new physicians who sold medical excuses to workers, so they could receive sick pay or early retirement, and then either not work or work privately for extra money. He also castigated the new teachers who for pay had privately tutored students, so they could advance faster than others who could not afford such services.[22] The legal system was called on to deal with these abuses.

As Castro has always made clear, only a minority of new professionals have engged in such abuses. But he expressed the fear that, if not stopped, such practices might spread and corrupt greater numbers of new professionals. He also worried that such practices could corrupt or demoralize workers, and undermine their commitment to hard work and their support for the revolutionary leadership and even for socialism. As will be seen in Chapter 7, in 1986 another rectification process was begun, which, among many other things, aimed to curb new professionals and others seeking material privileges.

Delimiting the role of the new professionals, however, has involved much more than merely curbing their ability to seek material gain. Most important, it has involved a clear definition of their spheres of responsibility and decision making in relation to the revolutionary leadership. Of course, the principles of democratic centralism do this, but only theoretically and very generally. An understanding of how the new professional role has been defined practically and specifically can be gained by examining how the revolutionary leadership has both encouraged and limited the powers of economic professionals since 1970.

With the new emphasis on economic studies, and the expansion of economic studies education after 1970, came new vehicles through which economic professionals could begin to express their professional concerns. For example, the first journal of the profession, *Economía y Desarrollo*, appeared in early 1970. According to the editor's introduction to the inaugural issue, this journal was to be "a medium for information and exposition of ideas by economic professionals, professors, students, workers in economic organizations and other comrades dedicated to work or study in this area of activity."[23]

Typical issues have featured an "Academicas" section, highlighting relevant academic events such as conferences, essay contests, special courses, professors visiting from abroad, and Cubans going abroad to study for advanced degrees; a "Cuba Económica" section, giving detailed information on the development of particular industries, the overall performance of the economy for a particular year, and the like; important official speeches and documents of economic relevance; and articles by Cuban professionals on a variety of topics. According to one count, in its first 12 years of existence, *Economía y Desarrollo* published 472 articles, 72 percent of which were written by Cubans.[24]

Although *Economía y Desarrollo* has been a forum for Cuban economic professionals, it has not seen anything like the "Great Debate" that raged in the Cuban journals of the early 1960s. Although the editors announced in the inaugural issue that they would publish, possibly with editorial comment, articles or ideas with which they did not agree, this seems never to have happened, The only instances of open debate have occurred when the editors have published an article by a nonsocialist-bloc author to which a Cuban then responded, and this occurred only in the early years of the journal.[25] Thus, the editors of *Economía y Desarrollo* have not provided a forum in which Cuban economic professionals could discuss the great issues of socialist construction. Rather, the editorial purpose behind *Economía y Desarrollo* seems to be to orient the new economic professionals to the path of socialist construction decided upon by the revolutionary leadership and to the operational problems with which this path has to contend.

In 1978 another major journal in this area appeared, *Cuestiones de la Economía Planificada*. Published under the auspices of the Central Planning Agency (JUCEPLAN), this journal carried articles considered relevant to the establishment of the Economic and Management System (SDPE) in Cuba. In its first two years, this journal published only articles by socialist-bloc, and especially Soviet, writers. Since Cubans had accumulated by 1980 some experience of their own with the SDPE, the journal was opened then to them as well. Specifically, the editorial board invited Cuban economic professionals to debate "practical questions" related to SDPE. As with *Economía y Desarrollo*, editorially *Cuestiones de la Economía Planificada* appears to be oriented to the ongoing system, not to debate on larger policy issues.[26]

Perhaps the most dramatic development for economic professionals was the founding of the National Association of Cuban Economic Professionals (Asociación Nacional de Economistas de Cuba—ANEC) in 1979. ANEC has a variety of stated objectives. First, it is to educate its members regarding the economic problems of the Third World, the experience of Soviet-bloc countries in socialist construction, and the crisis of the capitalist world system. Second, it is to help spread economic knowledge and an awareness of economic realities both to other professionals and to the trade unions. Third, it is to maintain relations with foreign professional associations of economists, send delegations to international conferences, and promote an internationalist spirit among Cuban economic professionals.[27]

But it was clearly no accident that the creation of ANEC coincided with the introduction of SDPE. As has been seen, the latter requires a large body of economically trained or at least economically aware professionals to run it. Moreover, as Humberto Pérez, then president of JUCEPLAN pointed out in 1978, the application of SDPE to Cuban conditions could by no means be merely an automatic process.[28] Many problems needed to be researched and solutions found. Although, as will be discussed below, Pérez clearly indicated that it would be inappropriate for economic professionals to debate the relative merits of SDPE—this being properly the concern and province of the revolutionary leadership— economic professionals were needed to run the system and to solve the myriad problems connected with its implementation.

Although SDPE was being discussed by the revolutionary leadership as early as 1973, the economic studies curriculum in higher education was not adjusted to train students in the specializations deemed necessary for the operation of SDPE until the 1977/78 academic year, and the first class fully schooled in the new curriculum was not graduated until 1982.

All economic professionals who left school prior to 1982 presumably lacked some skills required by the SDPE, or even an adequate understanding of the system. It seems that ANEC's overriding objective is to orient economic professionals to the SDPE.[29]

The creation of journals and an organization for economic professionals illustrates their importance in the eyes of the revolutionary leadership after 1970. Of course, as has been seen, neither of these is intended as a forum for debating the larger issues of socialism. Both are designed to orient economic professionals to the leadership's societal decisions and their implementation. In addition, however, the leadership has allowed economic professionals to use these vehicles to discuss certain limited professional concerns. A good example is the shift in the pedagogical philosophy behind economic training.

Until the late 1970s, the reigning pedagogical philosophy in Cuban higher economic studies shunned the proliferation of academic specialties in favor of producing generalist economic professionals able to work in various economic fields.[30] This philosophy was evident in the 1960s, when only two generalist degress were offered: A Licentiate in Economic Studies and a Licentiate in Public Accounting, the latter changed to a Licentiate in Economic Control at the height of the *fidelista* period.[31]

But this philosophy changed dramatically with the introduction of the SDPE in the late 1970s. Beginning with the 1977/78 academic year, students at the various institutes of economy could specialize in any of the following courses of study: accounting, finances and credit, economic policy, national economic planning, statistics, economy of work, economy of technical-material supply, economy of industry, economy of transportation, and economy of foreign trade. In addition to these, a program in the economy of tourism was initiated at the University of Matanzas. Programs in industrial engineering, with further subspecialties in organization of work, organization of production, and quality control, all with much economic content, were opened in the higher polytechnic institutes. A program in management of the socialist economy was offered by the superior institutes of management of the economy. And a program in economy of agricultural was begun in the superior institutes of agricultural sciences.[32]

It could be argued that the introduction of the SDPE required greater specialization. But Cuban economic professionals, through ANEC and such professional journals as *Economía y Desarrollo*, began complaining about overspecialization. In their view, the educational specialization introduced with the SDPE was both economically and politically damaging. They argued that, given the continuing scarcity of economically trained personnel, Cuba needed not economic specialists but generalists who could deal with a variety of problems in different occupational posts, and who could move from one to another as needed. In addition, they argued that overspecialization put Cuban economic professionals at a disadvantage in understanding and debating the various ideological currents in world economic thought.[33]

Some noted with embarrassment an incident at the Sixth Congress of the International Economics Association, held in Mexico in 1980, when a high-level official of the organization objected to the presence of the Cubans, who had professionally published little or nothing. Cuban economic professionals therefore called for more generalist training to gain international recognition for Cuban economic thought and thinkers.[34] Another Cuban economic professional pointed with chagrin to the poor performance of the Cuban delegation to the Second Congress of the Association of Third World Economists, held in Havana in 1981. In his view, the Cuban delegation evidenced

timidity, a product of lack of experience in the debate of papers and new ideas, and including, in some cases, perplexity before evidence for which we have not always formed our own indispensable criteria, and about which we are not always as systematic in our study as is required in order to present ourselves properly at international events. . . . [We have] a certain unconscious tendency to limit ourselves, even when it is not strictly necessary nor convenient, to a narrow area of possibilities in a chosen activity and, therefore, to measure ourselves inadvertently by what we ourselves generate, which signifies, in fact, that we treat ourselves with extreme benevolence.[35]

To overcome this inexperience, provincialism, and self-limitation to a chosen activity, this economic professional urged ANEC to work toward making more information available to Cuban economic professionals and creating conditions for more of them to collectively examine and debate common problems and aspirations with economic professionals from other countries. He called on ANEC to develop more extensive relationships with foreign economics associations and to arrange more frequent visits to Cuba by influential foreign economists, even perhaps such antipathetic figures as Milton Friedman.

In his view, Cuban economic professionals should be encouraged to study not only their own economy and those of other socialist countries, but they should also study bourgeois economics and economies. For, unless Cuban economic professionals could understand the operation of capitalism concretely rather than theoretically and abstractly, they could not hope to understand the economic problems of, nor offer aid to, Third

World countries attempting to develop in cooperation with foreign capitalist enterprises.[36]

Criticisms such as these have led to an at least partial return to the more generalist pedagogical philosophy of the pre-SDPE era. In 1980, certain programs of study, such as the Economy of Work and the Economy of Technical-Material Supply were abolished as separate entities and integrated as themes into the National Economic Planning training program. In 1983, a leading member of the revolutionary leadership suggested that narrow specialization had been merely a provisional measure. He stated that changes were under way in higher education to create professionals with a broader, more generalist, base of knowledge.[37]

This conflict may not yet be over, but its course so far has been illuminating. First, it illustrates that Cuban economic professionals have been able to use ANEC and journals such as *Economía y Desarrollo* to express at least limited professional concerns. Second, it illustrates that, perhaps especially when these concerns are linked to central revolutionary values—for example, economic dynamism, national prestige, and internationalism—Cuba's revolutionary leaders consider their expression legitimate and attend to them. Third, it illustrates that the expression of such concerns, as in this case, can result in concrete change.

Of course, as pointed out above, the revolutionary leadership clearly does not currently envision—through ANEC, journals, or any other vehicle—anything like the "Great Debate" of the early 1960s. The new professionals are expected to shy away from openly questioning the societal decisions, which revolutionary leaders reserve to themselves. Because it is one of the clearest and most extended expressions of this expectation, the statement made in 1977 by Humberto Pérez the head of JUCEPLAN then, is worth quoting at length. Speaking to students and faculty at the University of Havana's Institute of Economy about the type of research they should pursue in relation to SDPE, Pérez explained:

Of course, this work of yours should take place with full freedom. . . . Not only should you investigate or examine or submit to analysis that about which there has been no official pronouncement or about which you hear that for the moment no idea of making an official pronouncement exists, but you should also submit to study and examine those questions about which official pronouncements have been produced. . . .

Within the official pronouncements there are questions of principle and questions of how to implement these principles. About questions of principle, of course, about an elemental question of revolutionary discipline, neither seminars should be held or investigations made. But about questions of how to implement these principles, a form of aid to their better implementation is precisely that you examine, without limitations of any type, the implementation already made, even when these principles have the character of a law, or a decree, of a resolution of a Ministry, of a promulgation of any other type.[38]

Thus, while the revolutionary leadership encourages new professionals to evaluate and improve the implementation of its societal decisions, it seeks to prevent them from questioning these decisions. The latter are to remain the province of the revolutionary leadership itself.

In sum, managing the transition from old cadres to new professionals in intermediate-level occuptions has involved more than criticizing and removing the former while favoring and promoting the latter. Unable to replace the old cadres immediately, the revolutionary leadership has attempted to encourage old cadres to convert themselves into new professionals and has pursued a policy of gradual transition, which has perhaps been slowed further by old cadre resistance. At the same time, the revolutionary leadership has attempted to prevent the new professionals from parlaying their educational advantages into material privileges. Moreover, they are to implement the leadership's societal decisions, not question them. Although, as yet, the new professionals have exhibited no propensity to openly challenge the Cuban leadership, as will be seen next, many of them, along with others, have proven less than reliable implementers of the leadership's plans.

NOTES

1. Orlando Carnota, "Algunas ideas para mejorar el trabajo de dirección," *Economía y Desarrollo* 16 (Jan.-Feb. 1973), pp. 62–93. For other examples of this genre, some of which reach a slightly higher level of sophistication, see Emilio Fernández Caballero, "El tiempo del dirigente," *Economía y Desarrollo* 18 (July-Aug. 1973), pp. 92–111, and "Formación de cuadros," *Economía y Desarrollo* 27 (Jan.-Feb. 1975), pp. 111–35; Nery Suarez Lugo, "Notas sobre la evaluación de cuadros," *Economía y Desarrollo* 34 (Oct.-Dec. 1976), pp. 117–37.

2. Osvaldo Dorticós, "Formación de cuadros económicos-administrativos en la industria ligera," *Economía y Desarrollo* 4 (Oct.-Dec. 1970), p. 17.

3. Fernández Caballero, "El tiempo," pp. 101–102.

4. Ibid., p. 108.

5. Author's interviews SMT.80, HGO1.80, and AGO2.81.

6. Humberto Pérez, *Sobre las dificultades objetivas de la revolución: lo que el pueblo debe saber* (Havana: Editorial Política, 1979), p. 14.

7. Of course, proportions are impossible to determine. According to some I interviewed, SMT.80 and AGO1.81, most old cadres have overcome their

bureaucratic style. But according to others, ST2.80, CMS.80, and HITS.80, most have not.

8. Raúl Castro, "Three Speeches Against Bureaucracy," in Michael Taber, ed., *Fidel Castro Speeches, Vol. 2: Our Power Is that of the Working People* (New York: Pathfinder Press, 1983), p. 290.

9. Ibid.

10. "Sobre la política de formación, selección, ubicación, promoción y superación de los cuadros," in Primer Congreso del Partido Comunista de Cuba, *Tesis y resoluciones* (Havana: Editorial de Ciéncias Sociales, 1978), pp. 57–91. Also, see Resolution on Cadre Training, Selection, Placement, Promotion and Advancement Policy," in Second Congress of the Communist Party of Cuba, *Documents and Speeches* (Havana: Political Publishers, 1981), pp. 297–300; Fernández Caballero "El tiempo"; and Suarez Lugo, "Notas."

11. "Sobre la política de formación," p. 61.

12. "5th Congress of the Communist Youth League (UJC)," *Granma Weekly Review*, April 12, 1987, p. 5; and "Deferred Session of the 5th Central Committee Plenum," *Granma Weekly Review*, Oct. 4, 1987, p. 5.

13. Fidel Castro, "Speech on the 35th Anniversary of the Attack on the Moncada," *Granma Weekly Review*, Aug. 7, 1988, p. 4.

14. The estimate of 532,980 secondary school graduates by 1980 fits nicely with other available data from the same time period. First, as would be expected, the 532,980 figure falls below the 1979 figure of 844,300 for all employees, including old cadres, in nonmanual occupations. See Comité Estatal de Estadísticas, Dirección de Demografia, *Encuesta demografia nacional de 1979: principales características laborales de la población de Cuba* (Havana: 1981), p. 51. Second, as would be expected, the 532,980 figure falls below the number of individuals in the Cuban labor force with "at least 12 years of schooling," which, as explained in the note to Table 5.2, includes individuals without secondary degrees. Based on the data provided by Claes Brundenius, "Some Notes on the Development of Cuban Labor Force 1979–80," *Cuban Studies/Estudios Cubanos*, 13, 2 (Summer 1983), pp. 70, 74, the number of individuals with "at least twelve years of schooling" can be calculated as 746,928 for 1979.

15. The 147,150 figure is the author's computation based on data given in Brundenius, "Some Notes," pp. 70, 74. Due to lack of data on the number of graduates from certain higher education institutions, such as the Party's Nico López School, it is impossible to estimate accurately the number of higher education graduates remaining in Cuba using the method used in Table 5.2 to estimate the number of secondary school graduates.

16. The 844,300 figure is from Comité Estatal de Estadísticas, *Encuesta demografia nacional de 1979*, p. 51. The category used in this source is "nonmanual occupations," which is close to but not the same as my category of "intermediate-level occupations," because it includes the revolutionary leadership. Unfortunately, these data offer no way to separate out the revolutionary leaders. But since, at the very most, they might number 0.5 percent of the population, or about 5,000 individuals, the resultant distortion is negligible.

17. This latter estimate rests on the assumption that the "not specified" category from Table 5.3 is equivalent to the "no formal education" category given in the source for Table 5.4. Since the "no formal education" category is missing in the data for Table 5.3, this is a distinct possibility, but, of course, cannot be verified.

18. The rather substantial drop that takes place in these data when moving from the advanced secondary to the higher education background is most likely due to the fact that potential fathers with higher education were more likely to join the exodus from Cuba, taking their university-bound children with them. Thus, these data suggest that, if not for the exodus, their chances would have been much greater, those for potential fathers with more than primary education also higher, and those for potential fathers with primary education or less much lower.

19. Author's interviews HES1.80 and HES2.80.

20. Fidel Castro, "Revolutionary Consciousness and the Fight Against Corruption," in Taber, *Castro Speeches*, p. 341.

21. In 1982, Castro made the suggestion that this be done, and he verified in 1986 before the National Assembly that it was being done. See *Granma Weekly Review*, Jan. 12, 1986, p. 7.

22. For these examples, see *Granma Weekly Review*, July 6, 1986, p. 3; and July 13, 1986, p. 9.

23. Consejo de Redacción, "Introducción," *Economía y Desarrollo* 1 (Jan.–Mar. 1970).

24. Raúl León Torras, "Claustra del acto central por el Día del Economistas," *Economía y Desarrollo* 71 (Nov.-Dec.), p. 244.

25. See, for example, the article by the North American economist Mario Nuti, "Contra la ganancia," and the response by the Cuban Ricardo A. Hernández, "Contra la ganancia: un commentario," both in *Economía y Desarrollo* 8 (Oct.–Dec. 1971), pp. 3–8 nd 10–17, respectively.

I have been unable to locate three issues of the journal in any of the major collections in the United States, the most complete of which is in the library of the Center for Cuban Studies in New York City. However, perusal of the indexes for each of these missing issues seems to corroborate the lack of debate.

26. Consejo de Redacción, "Commentarios de la Redacción," *Cuestiones de la Economía Planificada*, 3, 1 (Jan.–Feb. 1980), pp. 10–11. From the few issues that I have been able to locate, this conclusion seems also to be the case with two journals that appeared in the mid–1980s: *El Economista* and *Cuba Económica Planificada*.

27. Asociación Nacional de Economistas de Cuba, "Constitutión," *Economía y Desarrollo* 52 (Mar.–Abril 1979), pp. 27–28.

28. Humberto Pérez, "Las obtención de la mayor eficiencia posible en el uso de nuestro recursos," *Economía y Desarrollo* 46 (Mar.–April 1978), pp. 167–97. For a similar discussion of the need for economic research in the implementation of SDPE, see Francisco Martínez Soler, "Fortalecer y equipar la

initiativa creador del propio professional," *Economía y Desarrollo* 43 (Sept.–Oct. 1977), pp. 166–77.

29. Of course, this objective was shared with other organizations, such as the National School of Economic Management discussed in Chapter 4.

30. For a statement of this philosophy, see Osvaldo Dorticós, *Discurso en el acto de presentación de los militantes del Partido del Instituto de Economía* (Havana: Editorial de Ciéncias Sociales, 1969), p. 26.

31. *Economía y Desarrollo* 5 (Jan.–Mar. 1971), p. 196; and *Economía y Desarrollo* 6 (April–June 1971), p. 240. Some minor specialization was introduced in 1972/73, when students who had completed only three years of the curriculum in Economic Control were allowed to graduate as management accountants or system analysts. See *Economía y Desarrollo* 8 (Oct.–Dec. 1971), pp. 222–25.

32. Alexis Codina Jiménez and Joaquín Fernández, "Apuntes en el XX aniversario del inicio de la formación de economistas," *Economía y Desarrollo* 71 (Nov.–Dec. 1982), pp. 25–27.

33. Ibid., pp. 31–33, 37. Perhaps as a consequence of overspecialization, a Cuban graduate student in Economy of Foreign Trade whom I interviewed in 1980 had been trained in the practicalities of Cuban foreign trade, but knew of neither the Marxist theoretical debate over "unequal exchange," nor its many world famous protagonists, such as Arrighi Emmanuel, Samir Amin, and Charles Bettleheim. Author's interview HGS.80.

34. Codina Jiménez and Fernández, "Apuntes," p. 37.

35. Torras, "Claustra del acto," pp. 235–36. For this congress, whose major topic was the "Economic Crisis and its Effects upon the Third World," see *Memoirs: Second Congress of the Association of Third World Economists* (Havana: Editorial de Ciéncias Sociales, 1982). Although the research of Cuban economic professionals on the international economy is beyond the scope of this discussion, it should be said that their work has at times been impressive. For representative examples, see the publication of the Center for the Investigation of the World Economy, *Temas de Economía Mundial*; and Fidel Castro's work, *The World Economic and Social Crisis* (Havana: The Council of State, 1983), written with the help of the Center and of the University of Havana's Institute of Economy.

36. Torras, "Claustra del acto."

37. Carlos Rafael Rodríguez, *Palabras en los setenta* (Havana: Editorial de Ciéncias Sociales, 1984), pp. 35–39; also, see Fernando Vecino Alegret, "La educación superior: sus objetivos y los metodos para lograrlos," *Cuba Socialista* 4–5 (Dec. 1982–Feb. 1983), pp. 3–33.

38. Humberto Pérez, "La obtención de la mayor eficiencia posible en el uso de nuestro recursos," *Economía y Desarrollo* 46 (Mar.-April 1978), pp. 167–69. One example of such research is that undertaken by the National Commission on the Management System of the Economy, which has many new professionals attached to it, engaged in a thorough-going evaluation of the SDPE. See "Con-

stituidos nueve grupos de trabajo de la Comisión Nacional del Sistema de Dirección de la Economía,'' *Granma*, Aug. 6, 1986, p. 3. Another example is the 291 new professionals who are engaged in evaluating investment projects for the "Central Group" planning body. See José A. López Moreno, "Report on the Fulfillment of the 1985 Plan for Economic and Social Development and the Objectives Set for 1986,'' *Granma Weekly Review*, Jan. 12, 1986, p. 4.

6

Bureaucratic versus Democratic Centralism in the Cuban Economy

"As far as salaries go, there is chaos all over the country," Fidel Castro exclaimed in mid–1986.[1] And as he and others made clear throughout that year, more was involved than merely salaries. Prices, credit, employment practices, administrative procedures, and many other aspects of the economy could be characterized as "chaotic." Beneath this seeming chaos, however, was a discernible pattern of behavior distorting the operation of the organizational structures and motivational mechanisms introduced after 1970. At least until 1986, when the revolutionary leadership launched another rectification drive that targeted it and other problems, bureaucratic centralist behavior was plaguing the Cuban economy.

All levels of Cuban society contributed to this plague. Bureaucratic old cadres, technocratic new professionals, many workers, and even revolutionary leaders were behaving and interacting with one another in a bureaucratic—rather than a democratic—centralist fashion. But each category engaged in this behavior to a different degree. For example, as will be seen, the incidence and intensity of bureaucratic centralism was on the whole probably much higher among old cadres than among new professionals.

The term bureaucratic centralism subsumes many kinds of behavior that deviate from democratic centralist practice.[2] All of them, however, can be organized into two categories of bureaucratic centralism, which I will call simply Type I and Type II. Type I bureaucratic centralism takes place when higher-level leaders unduly interfere in the decisions or responsibilities formally delegated to lower-level leaders in the second step of the democratic centralist process for making and implementing decisions. In this second step, as explained in Chapter 4, administrative leaders are to make a decision. More general or more important decisions are to be made by higher-level leaders, while less general or less important decisions are to be made by lower-level leaders. Type I bureaucratic centralism, then, occurs when higher-level leaders usurp the responsibilities of subordinate leaders. As will become clear, the immediate effect of such usurpations can be either "benign" or "malign," depending upon whether the affected lower level is immediately helped or hindered by the undue interference from above.

Type II bureaucratic centralism takes place when a higher administrative level unduly intefers with the responsibility of a lower level in the first or third steps of the democratic centralist process for making or implementing decisions. As was explained in Chapter 4, in the first step, the lower levels, down to the masses, are to collectively discuss the issue at hand. And in the third step, these levels are to participate actively in implementing decisions. Type II bureaucratic centralism, then, occurs when higher levels unduly interfere with lower-level participation in either the pre-decisionmaking stage of discussion or the post-decision-making stage of implementation. Again, as with Type I bureaucratic centralism, Type II can be either benign or malign, depending upon whether its immediate effect is to help or hinder the affected lower level.

Of course, the concepts of democratic and bureaucratic centralism are too general to determine at what point higher-level interference becomes undue. This can only be determined through analysis of the specific character and effect of higher-level interference in particular instances. Despite their generality, however, the concepts of democratic and bureaucratic centralism outlined above provide a useful framework to guide the specific analysis that follows here of bureaucratic centralism in the Cuban economy up to 1986. This framework helps illuminate the connections between seemingly unrelated, contradictory, or chaotic patterns of behavior. It also helps identify some of the major causes of these patterns, both the systemic ones that are always present in socialist economies as we know them and the sociohistorical ones that are only present in a given situation.

BUREAUCRATIC CENTRALISM IN CUBA: TYPE I— HIGHER LEVELS PREEMPTING LOWER-LEVEL RESPONSIBILITIES

In Cuba, Type I bureaucratic centralism begins at the very pinnacle of the revolutionary leadership, with Fidel Castro himself, and from there ripples down through all levels of the economic system. Castro has often spoken about his personal interventions to detect and solve problems at all levels of the economy; he has explained that he has a staff of ''twenty *compañeros* who constantly travel, visiting factories, hospitals, schools, *coordinating, helping everybody*, and they are not inspectors but people who go around assessing the situation and *coordinating one organ with another*.''[3] Elsewhere, Castro has boasted about how small his staff is.[4] The issue here, however, is not the size of Castro's staff, but the character of its work. The attempt, especially with no realistic chance for success, to coordinate everybody and everything from the pinnacle on an ad hoc basis is a bureaucratic centralist mode of operation par excellence.

This is made clear by the particularly harsh description of Castro's interventions offered by an emigre Cuban manager:

After he visits a production unit conditions and results improve for a while. He puts his finger on the sore spot. *It is Fidel's command* and the party cell means nothing, *the organizational structure means nothing*. Whatever Fidel says must be done. . . . Within a week of his visit to the Antillana steel mill, 1,200 bicycles and 20 buses were allocated to the plant. Who could do this but Fidel? . . . *Fidel erodes all economic plans*, he destroys them. He flouts any plan in order to resolve a given problem in the place he is visiting. The problem is fixed in a few days but it will crop up again within three or four months.[5]

This is clearly an overstatement, yet one that points up some of the consequences of Type I bureaucratic centralism. Such interventions may have a benign, if short-term, impact on a particular location. But one need only wonder where the 1,200 bicycles and 20 buses came from to realize that their loss could have a malign impact elsewhere.

Type I bureaucratic centralism, however, has not been limited to Castro and his twenty *compañeros*. It has also been evident throughout the Cuban economy, especially in the relationship between the higher state organs, most particularly the ministries, and the enterprises subordinated to them. As was seen in Chapter 5, with the new Economic Management and Planning System (SDPE) in the late 1970s, enterprises were to become semi-autonomous units. By 1980, however, it was evident that the ministries would not easily allow their enterprises the autonomy envisioned, and many complaints about ''excessive'' ministerial ''tutelage and paternalism'' began to be voiced.[6] In 1985, it was reported that ''while the central planning system reduces its directive indicators [to enterprises], the ministries increase them, and the intent of the reform is lost in excessive paternalism.''[7]

Ministries have behaved toward their enterprises in a bureaucratic centralist fashion in a variety of ways. For example, they have demanded excessive information from enterprises in order to keep close tabs on their operation. In 1980, Felino Quesada Pérez of the Central Planning Agency (JUCEPLAN) stated that, as of 1979, almost two-thirds of the SDPE enterprises were being commanded to collect and hand over statistical data that were not required by law and went far beyond what the National System of Statistical Information required.[8] Fully 75 percent of these demands came from central state organizations, mostly the ministries.[9] The situation had little improved by 1986, when Fidel Castro was moved to complain that "statistics continued to be a mountain of data of debatable usefulness."[10] Quesada Pérez claimed that the collection and dissemination of such statistics wasted both time and material resources, and deflected enterprise personnel from their proper concerns. As he pointedly asked: "Can an enterprise overwhelmed with so much information . . . really dedicate itself to deepening the analysis of its enterprise management?"[11]

Ministerial bureaucratic centralism, however, has not been limited to mere demands for information, but has involved undue interference in the finances and daily operation of enterprises. Quesada Perez gave some telling examples.[12] First, he reported the case of a provincial office of a ministry that, when it found itself without sufficient funds to meet its payroll, illegally extracted 80,000 pesos from the National Bank account of one of the enterprises subordinate to it, at a time when the enterprise owed the bank over 847,000 pesos in overdue loans. Second, he reported that many enterprise managers complained that ministerial authorities had ordered them not to declare their unneeded inventories superfluous. Although such ministerial orders lacked legal force, they nevertheless kept these enterprises from selling this unneeded material to other enterprises that could put it to socially useful purposes. Third, he reported that many enterprise managers complained that they could not enter into contracts for the sale of their products to other enterprises, again because of illegal orders from their ministries. Quesada Pérez reported that enterprise managers "frequently" asked him, "When are we going to have real enterprises?" "When will we have autonomous enterprises?" "When are we going to be able to make decisions in our enterprises?"[13]

Despite such complaints, however, it would be wrong to suppose that the bureaucratic centralism of higher authorities in Cuba has been solely malign for those subjected to it.[14] For, at the same time that higher authorities have hindered enterprises, they have also routinely bailed them out of difficulties. On the one hand, although the SDPE envisioned enterprises that would be financially responsible for themselves and to the National Bank, if enterprises had losses at the end of the year, the National Bank routinely covered them.[15] On the other hand, although SDPE enterprises were supposed to realize a profit within the confines of relatively stable prices, central price authorities were very willing to grant price increases to enterprises. They were so willing, in fact, that in 1986 Fidel Castro warned that the SDPE "could become a complete farce, as regards enterprise efficiency" if enterprises were allowed to continue attempting to solve their problems through price increases.[16] Moreover, often when enterprise managers could not get permission from higher authorities to raise prices as high as they would have liked, they resorted to gouging other enterprises through various subterfuges, such as demanding the price of a finished job when supplying only the materials.[17] In short, partially due to the benign bureaucratic centralism of the central authorities and partially due to the manipulations of some enterprise managers, both the budget and price constraints on enterprises were exceedingly soft in Cuba, at least until the revolutionary leadership launched its latest rectification effort in 1986.[18]

In Cuba, such weak constraints paved the way for a variety of problems, including corruption and, as will be seen below, labor hoarding. Unrestrictive budget and price constraints facilitated the efforts of some managers and others to divert "the people's property" to their and their buddies' personal ends. For, although they still needed to fear getting caught by higher authorities, corrupt managers and others did not need to fear also financially damaging the economic unit for which they were responsible nor overly upsetting its members.[19] It is thus not surprising that corruption apparently reached epidemic proportions, at least up to 1986.[20]

A closer look at the examples provided by Quesada Pérez shows that benign and malign Type I bureaucratic centralism, where higher levels usurped the responsibilities of lower levels, could also interact to subvert the purposes of the SDPE. When enterprises were robbed of funds for operating their plants or for paying their debts, or were prevented from acquiring funds through selling their excess inventories, it strengthened the incentive for their managers to acquire funds by seeking concessions from banking or price authorities. The same was true when enterprises were prevented from entering into contracts to sell their goods. Then they sometimes produced goods that no one wanted and that could not be sold; as a result, they might run up debts that could not easily be paid and from which they would try to get excused. Harmful interference by higher authorities, thus, encouraged enterprises to actively seek from them benign bureaucratic centralist remedies.

BUREAUCRATIC CENTRALISM IN CUBA: TYPE II— MANAGERS BY-PASSING WORKERS' PARTICIPATION IN PREPARING AND IMPLEMENTING PLANS

Bureaucratic centralism of the second type, in which a higher administrative level unduly interferes with the responsibility of a lower level to participate in pre-decision-making discussion or post-decision-making implementation in the first or third steps of the democratic centralist process, could exist at any level of the economy. But Type II bureaucratic centralism in Cuba has been most evident and most interesting to analyze in the enterprises and work centers (local subunits of enterprises) where managers and workers have interacted directly.

Although no one has claimed that workers exercise effective control over the higher levels of economic planning in Cuba, the scholars who have specifically studied the question all agree that, as a result of the organizational changes discussed in Chapter 4, the right of workers to discuss the basic production issues of their enterprises and work centers has increased substantially since 1970.[21] Still, it is clear that, at least before 1986, this form of worker participation did not reach the genuine, if limited, level envisioned for it in the democratic centralist model. As the "Resolution on the Economic Planning and Management System" of the Second Party Congress pointedly explained in 1980:

It has not been possible to achieve the desired level of workers' participation in the drawing up of plans for enterprises, either because the time for this was not programmed or because the meetings to discuss figures for controlling the plan were not properly organized. In some cases, the administration of the enterprise or local and central agencies failed to provide the workers' collectives with all the necessary information. Then, when the final figures were released, no explanation was given as to why their proposals were not accepted—which was usually due to difficulties with supplies or some technical problem.[22]

A little over five years later, Fidel Castro could still say that "until recently no progress . . . [has been] made to facilitate practical participation by all administrative levels and workers' collectives in designing the plan."[23] It is clear from the resolution quoted above that these problems stemmed from the negligence of both higher-level administrative personnel who failed to provide enterprises with information on time, or at all, and enterprise or work center managers who failed to see to it that time was provided for workers to carry out discussions. The malign bureaucratic centralist behavior of various administrative levels rendered this form of worker participation problematic, at least up to 1986. Even if not in all places at all times, this failure was general enough to draw attention from Party congresses and revolutionary leaders.

As with the first type of bureaucratic centralism, it would be wrong to suppose that Type II has been solely malign. Given that, in Cuba as in other socialist economies, something close to full employment is guaranteed and the labor market is tight,[24] managers have faced the problem of attracting and retaining workers who could easily switch to other places of employment. To meet their production quotas, Cuban managers have, therefore, often struck benign bureaucratic centralist deals with workers over the terms of their employment. Managers have often offered workers jobs that, while sometimes requiring intense periods of productive effort, overall required less effort and, at the same time, guaranteed an acceptable or even higher rate of pay than alternative employment. Fidel Castro complained in 1986 that managers, who had been enabled to do so by soft budget and price constraints, had "competed among themselves to get the best workers, paid the best salaries, were less demanding, played the role of populists, paternalists, what have you, making no demands."[25] In the aggregate and over the long run, such deals operated against the workers' and everyone else's broader interest in greater overall production and economic efficiency. But, on the local level and in the short run, such deals helped solve the immediate problem of many managers, and evidently appealed to many, if not all, workers.

The workers involved, of course, should not be viewed simply as passive recipients of managerial largesse.[26] Such managerial offers had to be acceptable to workers, who in return had to be willing to remain at their jobs and exert the minimum level of productive effort required. Workers knew that the labor market was tight, and, with this in mind, they could bargain with managers over the terms of employment. Many workers were thus likely to demand the benign bureaucratic centralist deals that many managers were willing to offer.[27] At least up to 1986, this form of "worker participation" was quite widespread in Cuba.

The revolutionary leadership, of course, never intended that workers should participate in securing payment for less than an acceptable level of work or even for no work at all.[28] It specifically, if not very successfully, attempted to reestablish work norms after 1970, in part to prevent just such practices. In the post–1970 period, work norms were supposed to be introduced in two phases. The first phase was to put into place "elemental" norms, based on records of how much workers had produced on particular jobs in the recent past and on timing workers on these jobs in the present. Since such records were typically gathered and kept by the management, and since workers could control the speed of their efforts while being timed, both work center managers and workers exerted considerable influence over the level at which these base norms were set. At least partially because both managers and workers gained immediate advantage by having these norms set at the lowest possible mark, elemental norms overall have been relatively low. They have been primarily a device for detecting and helping reduce or eliminate the effect of production interruptions, rather than low productivity.[29]

The second phase was to introduce "technical" norms, based on scientific studies, not just of individual jobs, but of work centers, enterprises, and even whole sectors of the economy. These studies were supposed to focus on all factors that negatively affected productivity, such as poor equipment, poor or late supplies, poor maintenance, poor planning, and poor organization of the work process.[30] Technical norms were supposed to be a device for reorganizing work and intensifying labor. But perhaps because of the resistance of managers and workers,[31] the first phase of fully introducing these elemental norms had yet to be completed by 1986 and the second phase of introducing technical norms had hardly commenced.[32] Therefore, it is only elemental norms and their many negative consequences that need be examined here.

A speech delivered by Raúl Castro in 1979 is worth quoting at length for its unusually graphic description of how the Cuban system of work norms has been manipulated for certain individuals' short-term benefit:

The fact is that there are many instances of lack of work discipline, unjustified absences from work, deliberate go-slows so as not to surpass the norms, which are already low and poorly applied in practice, so that they won't be changed because they are being more than met. . . . There are a good many instances today, especially in agriculture, of people one way or another pulling one trick or another, pulling the wool over their own eyes and harming themselves in the process and working no more than four or six hours, with the exception of canecutters and possibly a few other kinds of work. We know that, in many cases, heads of brigades and foremen make a deal with them to meet the norm in half a day and then go off and work for the other half for some nearby small farmer, or to go slow and meet the norm in seven or eight hours; or to do two or three norms in a day and report them over other days, too, days on which they don't go to work, either just to do nothing at all or to do something else that brings in some more money; or to surpass the norm in eight hours but report having worked for ten or twelve hours so as not to have the norm upped. . . . All this is detrimental to production, the costs of the enterprise, and the produce that should be meeting the needs of the people. And all these "tricks of the trade" in agriculture are also found in industry, transportation services, repair shops, and many other places where there's rampant buddyism; cases of "you do me a favor and I'll do you one," and pilfering on the side. . . . The weaknesses and negligence are the responsibility of managers and of all of us who have not set up the most adequate work and salary mechanism and have not known how to organize things and create a certain sense of political and work responsibility on the part of workers.[33]

Such manipulations played havoc with the principle of "to each according to work" and threatened to make the official wage scales meaningless. Low elemental norms often enabled workers to produce far beyond their production quotas and thereby rack up bonuses that would result in salaries equivalent to or in excess of those workers and even intermediate-level professionals with greater educational qualifications and therefore at higher notches on the official wage scales.[34] This, of course, operated as a disincentive for workers to improve their levels of education and probably demoralized at least some new professionals who had already done this.

In the words of one member of the revolutionary leadership, "the correct organization and norming of work, even in the elemental phase, should guarantee that disproportionate salaries that result in a disharmony and dislocation of the entire system are not produced."[35] Yet such disharmony would seem inherent in the system of elemental norms, given the way they are determined and their tendency to be set low. One, albeit roundabout, way to mitigate this problem would be to stretch official wage scales, as was done in 1980, to increase the distance between the base wages for different levels of jobs. But to eliminate the problem in this way would require raising wages for higher-level jobs far beyond what the revolutionary leadership has ever suggested and probably beyond what the Cuban people would easily tolerate.

Elemental norms being so low, coupled with benign bureaucratic centralism in the form of soft budget and price constraints that enabled managers to pay excessive wages, also encouraged managers to hoard labor. As Fidel Castro stated in 1986: "There's often a tendency, instead of going and telling the worker 'make a greater effort, meet your obligation' . . . to go about making things up, asking for more people."[36] And such practices extended beyond production workers to administrative personnel as well. According to one report, the 90,000 state administrative personnel in 1973 had increased to some 250,000 by 1984. As banking official Marcos Portal remarked, administrative employment had never swelled so much as under the SDPE.[37] Such practices slowed the accomplishment of the revolutionary leadership's policy of having old cadres displaced by or converted into new professionals: Administrators could hire new professionals while continuing to employ their old cadre "buddies." And this, of course, further weakened the incentive for such old cadres to convert themselves into new professionals through further education.

The machinations reported by Raúl Castro arose when elemental norms were used, or rather abused; but in many instances managers apparently did not even use these norms, except to complete some critical link in the production process or to fulfill a delayed plan. For the most part, especially in slow periods when there was little work to be done or in idle periods when production was interrupted because of weather, shortage of supplies, or lack of managerial foresight, many managers reverted to paying workers by time, not work produced, that is, guaranteeing workers their base wage as determined by their position on the official wage scale, regardless of how much work they actually performed.[38] Alternatively, although this was targeted for change in 1986, Cuban labor law allowed for workers to be paid 70 percent of their official wages by the state in the event of temporary layoffs made necessary by temporary production interruptions. But many managers apparently took advantage of this proviso to pay workers for longer periods of time and to keep a surplus labor force attached to their productive unit, that is, to hoard labor as protection against the vagaries of the tight labor market.[39] In other words, in order to keep workers attached to their economic unit, many managers saw to it that workers got paid, not for work performed according to norm, but simply for being on the payroll, available when needed.

To recapitulate, because of the malign bureaucratic centralism of administrative personnel, the ability of Cuban workers to participate in discussing the basic production issues of their enterprises and work centers, although substantially increased over what it had been in the 1960s, remained problematic, at least up to 1986. Cuban workers, however, were able to participate widely in bargaining with managers over the terms of employment. The tight labor market enabled workers easily to seek employment elsewhere. As a result, many managers, to attract, retain, and elicit productive effort from workers, resorted to striking deals with them that guaranteed less work at an acceptable or even higher pay level than alternative employment. In this way, at least up to 1986, a pattern of Type II benign bureaucratic centralism was established in Cuba between many managers and many workers.

SOME MAJOR CAUSES OF BUREAUCRATIC CENTRALISM

As indicated by the use of the term throughout the socialist world, bureaucratic centralist behavior takes place in all socialist economies as we know them. It can, therefore, be explained in part by "systemic" factors that, because they are inherently related to the structure and operation of the existing socialist economies, are always present. Still, the incidence and intensity of bureaucratic centralism varies among the different socialist economies and among the different types of economic actors within them at different times. Therefore, bureaucratic centralism must in part be explained by "sociohistorical" factors that are only sometimes present. From what has already been said, it is clear that the problem of bureaucratic centralism has for many years been quite severe in Cuba, and, as will be seen presently, more severe among some types of economic actors than among others. Thus, both systemic and sociohistorical factors must be sought to explain Cuba's plague of bureaucratic centralism.

The Hungarian economist Janos Kornai has identified the existing socialist relations of production themselves as a key systemic factor accounting for bureaucratic centralism.[40] The very fact of state ownership and central control of the major means of production encourages the revolutionary leadership to develop a sense of responsibility for the economy and for its various units. As a result, the incentive is strong for the leadership to intervene at any level of the economy, even down to the level of a particular work center, when it perceives that individuals at any of these levels are creating or not solving problems, or when it perceives that such individuals require help. Thus, what are here called the benign and malign varieties of Type I bureaucratic centralism stem in part from the system of production relations that exist in socialist economies.

What is true for revolutionary leaders also holds for administrative personnel at every level of the economy. At each level, administrators can be expected to develop what Kornai calls an "identification with their own job."[41] They can be expected to develop for their own economic unit and for the totality of those units subordinated to them a sense of responsibility, similar, although of narrower scope, to that of the leadership. This does not mean, of course, that each subordinate unit will be equally cared for at each point. Ministerial personnel, for example, may malignly intervene in certain enterprises in order to benignly help others or to protect what they perceive as the interests of their ministry as a whole.

Once in existence, the various types of bureaucratic centralism interact with one another, and bureaucratic centralism tends to become self-generating and self-reinforcing. First, when higher-level personnel engage in bureaucratic centralism, they create an example for lower-level personnel to emulate. Second, as has already been seen, when enterprises are put in jeopardy by the bureaucratic centralist interference of higher authorities, this strengthens their incentive to request compensatory benign interventions. Third, when managers strike benign Type II bureaucratic centralist deals with workers, they often do so out of identification with their own job, that is, out of a desire to protect the economic units they oversee from the vagaries of a tight labor market, another systemic characteristic of existing socialist economies. And, when higher authorities cover the expenses incurred, they in fact encourage such managerial behavior.

Fourth, if Type I bureaucratic centralism becomes commonplace, this may well stifle initiative at lower levels, which in turn can lead to further intervention from above. Although he reversed the causal sequence, Raúl Castro once described this connection quite vividly:

We often notice a certain rigidity in the cadres of our administrative aparatus and in the political and mass organizations. We should ask ourselves if, after twenty years of revolutionary power and in spite of our vast experiences in the affairs of politics and government, after structural improvement with the process of institutionalization, we are still not able to see to it that every worker and peasant, student or soldier, and every minister or state and party leader, knows exactly what his or her powers, obligations, and tasks are?

And if we answer this question in the affirmative, then why do so many pull back when they face problems and limit themselves to telling those nearest at hand that "things are rough" rather than immediately assuming responsibilities, be they those of a simple worker or those of an official or leader at any level?

After twenty years of revolution are we going to continue the widespread practice of waiting for somebody to push us to do our duty? Or to be quite clear: How long are we going to go on allowing unresolved problems to reach crisis point and then ask Comrade Fidel to take over the situation and pull our chestnuts out of the fire?[42]

Of course, Raúl Castro could have just as well asked how many called or waited for the intervention of, not just Comrade Fidel, but other members of the revolutionary leadership, the ministries, the banking, price, and other authorities. For, as has been seen, although bureaucratic centralism has started at the top, it surely has not ended there. But the central point here is that waiting for Fidel or for other members of the administrative apparatus has been clearly different than waiting for Godot: The former could be expected to show up. And so long as individuals knew this, they were likely to orient their behavior to it. They would often wait rather than take initiative, and their lack of initiative further encouraged higher-level personnel to intervene in a bureaucratic centralist fashion.

Bureaucratic centralism, then, arises in part from the proximate or mediate impact of systemic factors. But it also arises from sociohistorical factors.[43] The most obvious such factor in Cuba has been the multifaceted legacy of the experience of the 1960s, and especially of the *fidelista* period. That era of highly centralized decision making, in which workers had little voice, and in which the watchword was to mobilize for production rather than to debate problems or alternatives, formed hard-to-break bureaucratic habits in many administrative personnel. As was seen in the last chapter, Humberto Pérez remarked on the bureaucratic habits of many old cadres. But his remark could apply as well to the revolutionary leadership, which, although it has encouraged democratic centralist principles, has itself often engaged in bureaucratic centralist behavior. After 1970 the leadership indicated its genuine desire to move in a democratic centralist direction—although without giving up ultimate control through the system of interlocking positions in the Party and other organizations. But, in the immediate situation when problems emerged, it often responded, out of habit, in a bureaucratic centralist fashion.

Of course, the legacy of the 1960s is embodied most directly in the old cadres. They rose to positions of responsibility in that period, and they did so on the basis of political reliability rather than educational credentials and skills. Many of them have probably shunned the participatory first and third steps of the democratic centralist decision-making process, not only out of encrusted bureaucratic habit, but, recognizing their relative lack of skills, also out of distaste for or fear of opening up their decisions to lower-level and worker scrutiny. Furthermore, because of their relative lack of skills, many old cadres have doubtless had difficulty solving problems at their level without striking benign bureaucratic centralist deals with those below and without seeking bureaucratic centralist help from those above. Although bureaucratic centralist behavior has perhaps not appealed equally to all old cadres, it must have greatly appealed to those old cadres with the most bureaucratic habits and fewest skills.

By contrast, bureaucratic centralist behavior has probably attracted a smaller proportion of new professionals. They are more likely to have internalized the principles of democratic centralism, both because of their training and because these principles, as has been seen, justify their relative position and role in the decision-making process. Possessing educational credentials and presumed expertise, they no doubt have had more confidence in their decisions, and less fear of opening these up to lower-level scrutiny. With relatively greater skills, they are more likely to be able to solve problems at their own level without resorting to bureaucratic interactions with those above and below them.

Furthermore, with greater confidence in their skills and decision-making capacities, new professionals are more likely to resent and less likely to invite bureaucratic centralist interventions from above. Kornai has suggested that administrative personnel commonly have contradictory attitudes toward the benign bureaucratic centralist interventions of their superiors.[44] On the one hand, they often invite it, because it offers a measure of security in the face of adversity. On the other hand, they frequently resent it, because it robs them of their independence. The new professionals, given their greater skills and self-confidence, are likely to gravitate toward the latter.

This is not to say that Cuba's new professionals have been altogether immune to bureaucratic centralism. They have, of course, been subject to the same systemic factors that have pushed all Cubans toward such behavior. In addition, as seen in the last chapter, at least some of them might develop a technocratic consciousness that, among other things, would move them to arrogate to themselves, as experts, the right to make decisions without involving lower-level personnel in any of the democratic centralist decision-making steps. But for the reasons given above, bureaucratic centralist behavior is likely to appeal to a higher proportion of old cadres than of new professionals.

The apparently high incidence and intensity of bureaucratic centralism that plagued democratic centralist Cuba at least up to 1986, then, resulted from both systemic and sociohistorical factors. Most important among the latter was the legacy of the 1960s, which, among other things, gave rise to the old cadres who, with their encrusted bureaucratic habits and relatively few skills, continue to hold many intermediate-level posts. As the old cadres are either displaced by or convert themselves into new professionals, the incidence and intensity of bureaucratic centralism in Cuba may lessen somewhat. Of course, this also depends on the extent to which the revolutionary leadership succeeds in shaking its own bureaucratic habits and in forming new professionals with a democratic centralist rather than a technocratic consciousness. In addition, it depends on the extent to which workers fully develop a sense of collective responsibility that prevents them from participating in benign bureaucratic centralist deals with managers, something workers are likely to do only if they are allowed much greater participation in discussing basic production issues than has been the case in Cuba, at least up to 1986.

NOTES

1. Fidel Castro, "Let the Spirit of Militancy Be the Main Thing We Get Out of This [3rd CDS] Congress," *Granma Weekly Review*, Oct. 5, 1986, p. 9.

2. In Cuba and in the rest of the socialist world, behavior that deviates from democratic centralist practice is known by myriad terms, from "paternalism" and "tutelage" to "bureaucratic centralism." I prefer the latter term, because it contrasts nicely with democratic centralism and makes clear that it is from the latter that bureaucratic centralist behavior deviates.

Although this chapter focuses on the economy, bureaucratic centralism spreads beyond this sphere. It has been evident throughout the Cuban system, including the Organs of Popular Power (OPP). The *Second Congress of the Communist Party of Cuba: Documents and Speeches* (Havana: Political Publishers, 1981), pp. 346–52, after applauding the OPP for being an effective channel of popular participation in the state, noted that greater care had to be taken to ensure that higher bodies did not usurp the responsibilities of lower ones. The best and most detailed available non-Cuban scholarly analysis generally agrees that the OPP, while opening up the Cuban political system to more extensive and stable political participation, is itself riddled with limitations and problems, many of a bureaucratic centralist nature. See Carollee Bengelsdorf, "Between Vision and Reality: Democracy in Socialist Theory and Practice" (Ph.D. diss., Massachusetts Institute of Technology, 1985).

3. *Granma*, Feb. 11, 1985, pp. 14–15, as quoted in Sergio Roca, "State Enterprises in Cuba under the New System of Planning and Management (SDPE)", *Cuban Studies/Estudios Cubanos* 16 (1986), p. 174 (emphasis added).

4. Frei Betto, *Fidel on Religion* (Sydney, Australia: Pathfinder Press, 1986), p. 30.

5. Quoted in Roca, "State Enterprises," p. 172 (emphasis added).

6. *Segunda plenaria nacional de chequeo de la implantación del SDPE* (Havana: Ediciones JUCEPLAN, 1980), p. 405. Also see Julio A. *Díaz Vázquez, "La aplicación y perfeccionamiento de los mecanismos de dirección en la economía cubana," Economía y Desarrollo* 78 (Jan.-Feb. 1984), p. 94.

7. *Granma*, Feb. 16, 1985, as quoted in Roca, "State Enterprises," pp. 161–62.

8. Felino Quesada Pérez, "La autonomía de la empresa en Cuba y la implantación del sistema de dirección y planificación de la economía," *Cuestiones de la Economía Planificada*, 3, 1 (Jan.-Feb. 1980), p. 97.

9. *Segunda plenaria*, pp. 7–8.

10. Fidel Castro, "Main Report to the 3rd Congress of the Communist Party of Cuba," *Granma Weekly Review*, Feb. 16, 1986, p. 7.

11. Quesada Pérez, "La autonomía," p. 97.

12. Ibid., pp. 97–98. Roca, "State Enterprises," pp. 159–60, reports comparable examples involving ministerial interference with enterprise resources and planning.

13. Quesada Pérez, "La autonomía," pp. 95–96.

14. This is, in fact, one of the major mistakes of Sergio Roca, who has written one of the only other studies, cited above, of problems with enterprise autonomy under SDPE. He assumes that higher-level interference typically only impacts negatively on enterprises. Here the elite/mass dichotomy conceals the fact that the direction of influence between higher authorities and enterprise managers goes both ways. He might have seen that enterprise managers, as discussed farther on, have not only sometimes bristled under malign bureaucratic centralism but have sometimes invited benign bureaucratic centralism from those above them, or even needed such interventions because of their irresponsibility.

15. See, for example, Fidel Castro, "Speech at the 25th Anniversary of the Committees for the Defense of the Revolution," *Granma Weekly Review*, Oct. 6, 1985, p. 4; Fidel Castro, "Speech at the Close of the Deferred Session of the 3rd Congress of the Communist Party of Cuba," *Granma Weekly Review*, Dec. 14, 1986, p. 12; and "Debates on Rectification of Errors and Negative Tendencies in Various Spheres of Society at the Deferred Session of the 3rd Congress of the Communist Party of Cuba," *Granma Weekly Review*, Dec. 4, 1986, p. 12.

16. Castro, "Main Report," p. 7. Roca, "State Enterprises," pp. 162–63, quotes emigre ex-enterprise managers who claimed that price constraints on enterprises were overly harsh in the late 1970s. Perhaps so, but the situation certainly reversed in the 1980s. As Fidel Castro complained about the extent of benign Type I bureaucratic centralism in 1986, "I've come to the conclusion that we've become a paternalistic state, that we've been too protective, too generous, too splendid and magnanimous, and that elements who should be ashamed of themselves have taken advantage of the state's magnanimity." "Report on Fidel Castro's Speech on Administrative Irregularities in Economic Management at the National Assembly," *Granma Weekly Review*, July 13, 1986, p. 9.

17. Castro, "Speech at the Close of the Deferred Session," p. 11; also, see his "Speech to the Closing of the 9th Session of the National Assembly," *Granma Weekly Review*, Jan. 12, 1986, p. 10; and "Report on Fidel Castro's

Speech at the 25th Anniversary of the Proclamation of the Socialist Nature of the Revolution," *Granma Weekly Review*, April 27, 1986, p. 10.

18. Janos Kornai underscores the importance of what he calls "soft" budget and price constraints; he has put them at the center of his comparative theory of capitalist and socialist economies. See his *Economics of Shortage* (Amsterdam: North-Holland, 1980), chap. 13; and his *Contradictions and Dilemmas* (Cambridge: Massachusetts Institute of Technology Press, 1986), chap. 2.

19. Of course, some enterprise members did get upset, like Silvia Marjorie Spence—now famous in Cuba—who was fired from her construction work center for complaining about rampant corruption, in this case contracts for nonexistent jobs and incredibly high monthly salaries by Cuban standards: one of 1,246 pesos, one of 1,013 pesos, four over 900, and four over 800. "Report on Fidel Castro's Analysis of the Economic Situation and the Essential Measures to Be Taken," *Granma Weekly Review*, Jan. 11, 1987, p. 4. She was reinstated over two years later, but only after having taken her case to the national level. She has now been promoted to the status of a hero, while her former superiors have been demoted to the shop floor. See "New Hero: Whistle-Blower Silvia Marjorie Spence," *Cuba Update*, 8, 1–2 (Spring 1987), p. 7. For more on the problem of corruption, see "Report on Fidel Castro's Speech at the Meeting to Analyze Enterprise Management in the City and Province of Havana," *Grahma Weekly Review*, July 6, 1986, p. 2; and Castro, "Let the Spirit of Militancy," p. 4.

20. Although clearly secondary to that in the state sector, corruption also became a major problem in areas where centrally controlled price and budget constraints did not operate, such as the "free farmers' markets." See Medea Benjamin et al., *No Free Lunch: Food and Revolution in Cuba Today* (San Francisco: Institute for Food and Development Policy, 1984), chap. 5; and Fidel Castro, "Closing Speech at the 2nd National Meeting of Agricultural Production Cooperatives," *Granma Weekly Review*, June 1, 1986.

21. Andrew Zimbalist, "Workers' Participation in Cuba," *Challenge*, (Nov.-Dec. 1975), pp. 45–54; Marifeli Pérez-Stable, "Institutionalization and the Workers' Response," *Cuban Studies/Estudios Cubanos*, 6, 2 (July 1976), pp. 31–54; Marifeli Pérez-Stable, "Politics and Conciencia in Revolutionary Cuba, 1959–1984" (Ph.D. diss., State University of New York at Stony Brook, 1985); Alejandro Armengol Ríos and Ovidio d'Angelo Hernández, "Aspectos de los procesos de comunicación y participación de los trabajadores en la gestión de las empresas," *Economía y Desarrollo* 42 (July-Aug. 1977), pp. 156–79; Antonio José Herrara and Hernan Rosenkranz, "Political Consciousness in Cuba," in John Griffiths and Peter Griffiths, eds., *Cuba: The Second Decade* (London: Writers and Readers Cooperative, 1979), pp. 36–52; Marta Harnecker, *Cuba: Dictatorship or Democracy?* (Westport, Connecticut: Lawrence Hill, 1980); Linda Fuller, "The Politics of Workers' Control in Cuba, 1959–1983: The Work Center and the National Arena" (Ph.D. diss., University of California at Berkeley, 1985); and her "Changes in the Relationship among the Unions, Administration, and the Party at the Cuban Workplace, 1959–1982," *Latin American Perspectives*, 13, 2 (Spring 1986), pp. 6–32.

22. *Second Congress*, p. 387. For further evidence of these problems, see Hector Anala Castro, "Transformación de propriedad en el período 1964–1980," *Economía y Desarrollo* 68 (May-June 1982), pp. 23–24; and Díaz Vázquez, "La aplicación," pp. 92–93.

23. Fidel Castro, "Main Report," p. 7.

24. Calling the Cuba labor market "tight" does not imply that there is an absolute labor shortage in Cuba. First, as Kornai, *Economics*, pp. 30–36 and 254–57, has fully explained, a tight labor market can go hand in hand with a labor surplus within all enterprises, or what is sometimes called "unemployment on the job." Second, while there is a relative labor shortage in most of Cuba, in fact, according to Fidel Castro, there is "a certain labor surplus" in Eastern Cuba. See "Report on Fidel Castro's Analysis," p. 4. Interesting enough, he had complained several months before about the difficulties of a new textile mill in Santiago, that is, in the labor-surplus East, to attract workers, because it did not have the housing, recreational, educational, and other facilities that workers demanded. See "Report on Fidel Castro's Speech on the 25th Anniversary," pp. 10–11. In between these two statements, Castro explained that many workers on temporary lay-off were reluctant to go elsewhere for work, because they were receiving 70 percent of their salary while not working. "Cuban Television Broadcasts Key Parts of Fidel's Remarks at 2nd Central Committee Plenum," *Granma Weekly Review*, Aug. 3, 1986, p. 5. Together, these statements suggest that in Cuba the labor market remained tight, even where a labor surplus existed, because of the high level at which the state guaranteed the livelihood of workers.

25. Fidel Castro, "Speech at the Close of the Deferred Session," p. 12.

26. It is notable in this regard that, in the mind of one Party member, the behavior of work center managers, about to be discussed, stemmed from the fact that "people in authority do not want problems and some are afraid of workers." See the remarks of Reinaldo Marsilli, as reported in "Debates on Rectification," p. 3. It is also notable that, as pointed out in Chapter 4, note 9, the workers interviewed by Fuller, *Politics*, pp. 423–25, felt they had the power to have work center managers removed, if necessary.

27. See, in this regard, Fidel Castro's remark about "the increase in the ambition for money, the spirit of profit that was invading our working class." "Report on Fidel Castro's Speech at the Meeting," p. 2.

28. As Fidel Castro admitted in 1986: "We abused the principle [of pay according to work] by paying for work not done." "Report on Fidel Castro's Speech at the Meeting," p. 3.

29. Alexis Codina Jiménez, "Los estimulos materiales y morales en el socialismo," *Economía y Desarrollo* 56 (Mar.-April 1980), pp. 60–61.

30. According to one Cuban commentator, technical norms "are not limited to passively reflecting the costs of work and the results that should be expected from each post of work, brigade, etc., but should exercise an active influence in the transformation of the general conditions and organization of work." See Codina Jiménez, "Los estimulos," p. 61.

31. While in 1986 there were about 3 million work norms and about 20 thousand norm setters—that is, about 150 norms per norm setter—these latter often lacked proper training or experience, or often did other work, perhaps as directed by managers. See the remarks of the president of the State Committee for Labor and Social Security, Francisco Linares, "Debates on Rectification," p. 2. Of course, even with thoroughly trained and cooperative personnel, establishing and keeping this many norms up to date in the face of a complex division of labor and changing technology, work organization, and worker performance would be an enormous task. Therefore, in addition to managerial and worker resistance, the technical problems involved also help account for the well-known problems with systems of work norms that have plagued not only the Cuban but other socialist economies. Discussing these technical difficulties here would take us too far afield.

32. As early as 1972, then Minister of Labor Jorge Risquet announced that elemental norming would be complete by the end of 1973 and extensive technical norming would commence. See "Primer encuentro nacional de organización y normación del trabajo," *Economía y Desarrollo* 11 (May-June 1972), p. 200. But, by 1981, almost 28 percent of the appropriate work posts remained without norms of any kind. See Barbara Flores Casamayor, "Breve analisis del sistema salarial, en los marcos de la Reforma General de Salarios," *Economía y Desarrollo* 78 (Jan.-Feb. 1984), p. 119. And, by 1982, 77 percent of all existing norms remained elemental, practically none were technical, and 23 percent were somewhere in between. See María Díaz Corral and Xionmara Vásquez Grau, "Algunas consideraciones para la aplicación de reglamento de normación del trabajo," *Economía y Desarrollo* 85 (Mar.-April 1985), p. 227. This situation had not substantially improved by 1986. See the remarks of Fidel Castro, "Main Report," p. 6.

33. Raúl Castro, "Three Speeches Against Bureaucracy," in Michael Taber, ed., *Fidel Castro Speeches., Vol. 2: Our Power Is that of the Working People* (New York: Pathfinder Press, 1983), pp. 295–96. For a report of similar manipulations, see "Debates on Rectification," p. 3.

34. See "Report on Fidel Castro's Speech on Administrative," p. 9. One study of 85 enterprises in the province of Ciego de Avila discovered 2,442 workers being overpaid, and attributed this to the low work norms found in 32 enterprises, in 28 of which workers were producing at the rate of more than 130 percent of their norms. See "Inspección a 85 empresas avileñas," *Granma*, Aug. 8, 1986, p. 1.

35. Raúl García Pelaez, untitled speech at the closing of the II Reunión Nacional de Checquo y Control de la vinculación del salario a la norma, *Economía y Desarrollo* 36 (July-Aug. 1976), p. 208.

36. "Report on Fidel Castro's Speech at the 25th Anniversary," p. 10.

37. "Report on the Meeting to Analyze Enterprise Management," p. 2.

38. García Pelaez, pp. 202, 207–8; and Humberto Pérez, "La obtención de la mayor eficiencia posible en el uso de nuestro recursos," *Economía y Desarrollo* 46 (Mar.-April 1978), p. 188.

39. "Debates on Rectification," p. 3.
40. Kornai, *Economics*, p. 566. Although there is a vast literature on socialist economies that deals with the types of problems analyzed in this chapter, I find Kornai's work most useful because, in my opinion, it presents the most impressive and systematic model of the operation of socialist economies that is available. The analysis of this chapter, however, differs from Kornai's in several respects. First, for the reason explained earlier in the text, this analysis uses the term "bureaucratic centralism" to refer to what Kornai calls "paternalism." Second, this analysis distinguishes between malign and benign paternalism or bureaucratic centralism, whereas Kornai's work does not distinguish the two, and in fact deals almost solely with the benign type. Third, this analysis uses the terms "systemic" and "sociohistorical" factors to refer, respectively, to what Kornai, *Economics*, pp. 62–63, calls "general" and "special" factors. Kornai's terminology creates confusion, because it can be easily seen that the special factors that he alludes to and the sociohistorical ones that I invoke here have existed "generally," that is, in most, perhaps all, existing socialist economies at one time or another, even though they have not arisen systemically from the structure or operation of these economies. Fourth, and most important, this analysis differs from Kornai's in its level of abstraction. Kornai theorizes primarily at the higher level of abstraction suitable to his overriding purpose of comparing capitalist and socialist economies, the essential difference between which he locates in the relationship, typically paternalist in socialist economies and typically nonpaternalist in capitalist economies, between the state and the enterprise.

Although his theoretical project is obviously moving in this direction, in his writings so far he has only minimally been interested in comparing the degree of paternalism or bureaucratic centralism in different socialist economies, at different points in time, and among different categories of economic actors. His theory in this respect is still incomplete and in flux. In his *Economics*, chap. 22, he theorizes that the degree of paternalism or bureaucratic centralism will be higher in pre-reform than in post-reform socialist economies. But he later offers counterfactual evidence in his *Contradictions*, pp. 81–123, where he suggests that very extensive reforms in Hungary did not appreciably reduce paternalism or bureaucratic centralism in that country's economy.

In treating the particular case of Cuba, the analysis of this chapter necessarily operates at a much lower level of abstraction, which accounts for its central difference from Kornai's analysis. Obviously, at the lower level of abstraction where a particular case is being analyzed, special or sociohistorical factors, such as the peculiarities of the different categories of economic actors invoked in this analysis, have to be called upon. In addition, I would suggest that, if Kornai is to fully develop a theory of degrees of paternalism or bureaucratic centralism in different existing socialist economies and among different types of economic actors at different times, he will have to take into consideration not just general or systemic but also special or sociohistorical factors.

41. Kornai, *Economics*, p. 62. In Kornai's view, this is an important *general* factor behind bureaucratic centralism, but, unlike state ownership of the major means of production, it extends in its generality to "*every* [that is, capitalist and socialist] modern, achievement-oriented society." See his *Contradictions*, p. 70.

42. Raúl Castro, "Three Speeches," p. 291.

43. No more than a hypothetical status can be claimed for our analysis of sociohistorical factors. It is composed of a series of hypotheses that fit my observations in Cuba, and it is supported by much of the data and analysis offered in this book. But to verify these hypotheses would require an empirical research project that included both careful observations and systematic interviews. As every Cuba scholar knows, and as Pérez-Stable, *Politics and Conciencia*, has most thoroughly discussed, for a variety of reasons, it is virtually impossible for a Cuba scholar from the outside to execute such a project there. The inability to verify these hypotheses is regretable, but hardly worthy of apology. Cuba scholars may hope for improved access, but they cannot refrain until they have it from drawing conclusions, however hypothetical. It is for the community of such scholars to judge whether these conclusions fit and advance our current state of knowledge.

44. Kornai, *Economics*, pp. 566–67.

7

Conclusion: Further Development of New Professionals in Cuba

The claim made here that Cuban studies would benefit from moving beyond the elite/mass perspective to admit intermediate strata and workers into the circle of politically relevant actors could be justified in Chapter 1 only with general considerations. It was argued that only by taking this new direction could Cuban studies hope to comprehend what actually happens in Cuban society at any particular time rather than merely what the revolutionary leadership wants to happen. Now the concrete results of the analysis in this book can bolster this claim. But first it is necessary to bring our account up to date by examining the leadership's latest attempt at rectification of Cuba's economic and political structures.

THE NEW ROUND OF RECTIFICATION SINCE 1986

Cuban leaders had begun speaking out against many manifestations of bureaucratic centralism and related problems in the late 1970s. But not until 1986 did they target these with a major rectification drive that, among other things, would speed the decline of the old cadres and the rise of the new professionals. Three reasons would seem to account for this delay. First, Fidel Castro claimed in 1987 that the leadership had been distracted from sufficiently attending to these problems by the need to build up the defenses of the country in the face of an increasingly hostile U.S. administration.[1] Second, it was apparently not until the mid–1980s that the Soviets began to voice their unwillingness to cover the increasing costs of economic inefficiency in Cuba.[2] Third, until the mid–

1980s the revolutionary leadership reasonably considered many of these problems to be part of an inevitable process of adjustment to new mechanisms, such as the Economic Management and Planning System (SDPE), and therefore as temporary.[3]

By 1986, however, it became clear that Cuba's economic problems were steadily worsening. Although the overall growth rate continued at a level considered acceptable by the revolutionary leadership, growth rates in export and import substitution industries were sluggish.[4] In addition, several years of drought, hurricanes, low international sugar prices, and a variety of other external factors over which the Cubans had no control, took their toll. All of these affected Cuba's hard currency balances, and in 1986 the country was for the first time unable to meet its foreign debt obligations and had to dramatically reduce its imports from the capitalist world. Perhaps most indicative of the fact that changes were in order, certain standard of living indicators started to deteriorate,[5] and the cost per unit of production, which had dropped slightly from 1981 through 1984, subsequently began to rise, as a result of excessive wage and materials expenditures by enterprises.[6]

No longer able to ignore these problems, in 1986 the Cuban leadership launched a drive to rectify, but not to jettison, the major organizational structures and motivational mechanisms that it had introduced after 1970. As will be seen, key elements of the post–1970 system, such as the SDPE, however modified, were to remain in place. In addition, the revolutionary leadership would push to speed the decline of the old cadres and the rise of the new professionals, even as it criticized more vociferously than ever the technocratic elements among the latter. In essence, the new rectification process since 1986 has focused on eliminating, not the system of the post–1970 period, but the bureaucratic centralist behavior and other problems that had been distorting its operation.

In late 1986, Fidel Castro sounded a theme to become characteristic of this new rectification process when he proclaimed: "A consciousness, a communist spirit, a revolutionary will and vocation were, are, and always will be a thousand times more powerful than money."[7] Through 1986 and early 1987, Castro offered four related justifications for this claim. First, he noted that material incentives were inapplicable to many occupations. In one of his favorite examples, if surgeons were remunerated according to the number of operations they performed, their incomes would soar and their incentive to perform needless, even harmful, operations would be strengthened.[8] Second, Castro maintained that material incentives were simply not as potent as moral ones for motivating individuals to do what was in the general social interest. A soldier, for example, might lay down his or her life for national dignity but hardly for a few extra pesos.[9] Third, he pointed out that misusing or overusing material incentives results in extreme distributional inequality, characteristic of capitalism but unacceptable under socialism.[10] Fourth, Castro damned the overuse of material incentives as encouraging selfishness, greed, and corruption, while undercutting political consciousness and commitment to the general welfare.[11]

Although all of this echoed statements he had made in the late 1960s, Castro was by no means calling for a return to the *fidelista* period, which he and other revolutionary leaders still considered a period of idealistic illusions.[12] Instead, he was calling for a return to balance in the incentive system, a balance he suggested had begun to be lost in the early 1980s. It was in 1980, the reader will remember from Chapter 4, that some restrictions on small-scale private enterprise were relaxed; that the General Wage Reform, which stretched the official wage scales and put greater emphasis on bonuses, was promulgated; that the SDPE, riddled with bureaucratic centralist practices, was extended to virtually all enterprises; and that the presumably morally motivated microbrigades for construction were eliminated. Since 1986, the rectification process has targeted each of these areas.

Material incentives were cut back initially in early 1986, when the revolutionary leadership drastically curbed small-scale private enterprise and abolished the free farmers' markets. The latter were abolished because, even after restrictions had been placed on them in 1982, it was claimed that they continued to suffer from corruption and profiteering. Moreover, the high profits that these markets provided some farmers kept them from joining the cooperative movement that the revolutionary leadership had been pushing for a decade. The population continued to resent the high incomes realized by some sellers on these markets—astronomical annual incomes of 100 to 300,000 pesos have from time to time been mentioned in the Cuban press—and the high prices they charged. As Fidel Castro pithily put it: "The people bought but they felt they had been robbed."[13]

Material incentives were further reduced in December 1986, when, to help contend with the country's economic crunch, the revolutionary leadership introduced a moderate austerity program. Among other things, the assignment of state-owned cars, per diem payments to government officials, and foreign travel budgets were cut back, while charges for public transportation, consumer utility use, and some parallel market goods were increased.[14] Partly to relieve the burden of these measures on the lowest paid workers, Fidel Castro soon called for those at the bottom of the official wage scales, 85 pesos per month, to get an increase to 100 pesos.[15] In calling for this increase, Castro criticized the 1980 General Wage Reform as the creation of those "who have nothing in common with the modest worker."[16] He went on to explain that, although strict egalitarianism was still not possible in Cuba, stretching the wage scales too much was intolerable and resembled capitalism.

This increase in the lowest wages was to be financed by savings realized through better application and enforcement of work norms. In other words, the socialist principle of "to each according to work," which had been originally promulgated in 1973, was now to be properly applied so that it could no longer lead to payment—that is, overpayment—for little or no work. To this end, Party members were mobilized against those work center managers who tried to elicit worker cooperation through the types of bureaucratic centralist deals discussed in the previous chapter. To prevent managers from hoarding labor, the revolutionary leadership began setting up in each work center a commission, headed by a Party representative, to take over the responsibilities of hiring and firing workers.

Reportedly, these efforts have had some success. Fidel Castro, for example, has praised the accomplishments of the Party in reducing the number of workers needed through properly applying norms in selected new work centers, such as the Guanabacoa bathroom fixtures factory, where the work force was reduced from 1,900 to 1,100.[17] But the revolutionary leadership has also recognized that fully correcting these problems will take many years. First, it has acknowledged that many managers continue to resist the proper use of work norms.[18] It was, in fact, probably out of frustration with this resistance that many of the bureaucratic centralist behaviors of managers, which Fidel Castro had first dubbed "mistakes," were later branded by him as "anti-social, criminal activities" and "acts of disloyalty."[19] Second, the revolutionary leadership knows that, while it can try to establish a workable system of norms for new work centers, it cannot all at once correct the problems in existing work centers. This would induce massive unemployment and probably lead to a major political crisis between the leadership and its working class supporters.[20] Ultimate success in this area, therefore, requires creating more jobs through economic expansion.

Fidel Castro has explained several times since 1986 that, in the current situation, Cuba can expect neither any assistance from the capitalist nor further assistance from the socialist countries; therefore, it must improve the overall efficiency of its economy and the operation of the SDPE for such an expansion.[21] As a result, in 1986 a national commission was set up to analyze the SDPE, and to propose solutions to the many problems with its operation. In the same year, Castro announced a hardening of the budget and price constraints on enterprises. He reported that the National Bank would no longer automatically bail out unprofitable enterprises, which one estimate put at over one-third of all the enterprises in the country.[22] Moreover, he attacked the tendency to solve problems with price increases where administrative mechanisms would be more appropriate. He castigated, for example, those who had raised prices on highway transport in order to help build up the railroads, when they could have simply ordered certain agencies to increase their rail use.[23] In general, although the SDPE was to remain in place, its operation was attacked for encouraging the misuse and overuse of material incentives and market mechanisms, and for failing to use moral incentives and political mechanisms.

One of the more obvious ways in which moral incentives have been reemphasized in the rectification process since 1986 has been through the reintroduction of the microbrigades.[24] These brigades of voluntary workers in construction had fallen out of use after 1980. Because their salaries were paid by the enterprises with which they were associated, they were considered at that time incompatible with the requirement that SDPE enterprises realize a profit. To make them compatible with the SDPE, in 1986 the state began paying enterprises for the salaries of their absent brigade members. By the end of 1987, Havana was expected to have about 30,000 microbrigade members, who would address, among other things, the deteriorating housing situation in that city. Beginning in 1988, microbrigades were to be created across the country.

The revolutionary leadership has also reemphasized moral incentives by exhorting everyone to raise their revolutionary consciousness and to let the general social interest guide their behavior. In addition, it has called on administrative personnel not to try to buy the cooperation of others with material incentives but to engage in political work. This does not mean, as Fidel Castro has pointed out,[25] that administrative personnel should merely mouth slogans and passages from Marx and Lenin, as had the old cadre chatterers. Instead, it means that, besides giving a good example themselves, they should motivate others by appealing to their political consciousness.

Finally, the revolutionary leadership has attempted to mobilize workers through their trade unions and under the direction of the Party to seek solutions to the problems of the SDPE and to expose the administrative personnel partially responsible for them. Although rejecting the desirability of a ''cultural revolution'' that would ''throw the people against those responsible," the leadership has called on workers to help the Party resolve the problems of the SDPE in an "organized and disciplined manner."[26] Although recognizing that some workers have participated in creating these problems, the leadership has not blamed them so much as the administrative personnel involved. As Fidel Castro declared in mid–1986: "The workers are not to blame for this. The guilty ones are the leadership personnel, the administrative personnel."[27]

Since 1986, workers and the wider population have been involved in the rectification process in a variety of ways. During that year, for example, the leadership submitted the Party program to the population for discussion, including the detailed operating principles of the SDPE. In the process, the people not only learned more about how the SDPE was supposed to work, but were able to criticize its application and operation in Cuba. Later, Fidel Castro called for worker and trade union participation in uncovering why so many enterprises were unprofitable, even though some of those that were not realizing a profit were well run.[28] In addition, the leadership has reportedly begun to address some of the problems mentioned in the last chapter with workers' participation in discussing the basic production issues of their enterprises and work centers. As a sign of this, in 1986 it was announced that, perhaps for the first time, planning authorities had delivered the requisite figures to all enterprises early enough for workers to discuss them.[29] Moreover, the leadership has accelerated the introduction of the system of "permanent and comprehensive brigades," which gives small groups of workers control over the means of production and the wage fund assigned to them, and responsibility for plan fulfillment and cost-accounting in their area.[30]

What impact has the rectification process begun in 1986 had on the old cadres and new professionals, and what impact is it likely to have in the future? A superficial appraisal might suggest that the reemphasis on moral incentives and political work would favor the old cadres over the new professionals and perhaps reverse the decline of the former. Yet, as was seen in the last chapter, the tendency to engage in bureaucratic centralist behavior would seem to be quite strong among the old cadres as a whole. And it has been these behaviors that, among other things, this rectification process has specifically targeted for elimination.

In fact, this rectification drive should altogether hurry the decline of the old cadres. It was announced that in Havana Province by December 1986 more than 400 administrative personnel, including 120 enterprise and work center managers, had been removed from their posts, as had 85 grass-roots Party leaders, because of their unwillingness or inability to change their behavior.[31] The analysis of this book suggests that, although some of these may have been new professionals, the majority were probably old cadres. If so, it would possibly signify that the policy of gradual transition from an administrative apparatus dominated by old cadres to one filled by new professionals was jettisoned in 1986 in favor of a rapid purge to speed the disappearance of the old cadres and the rise of the new professionals.

Such a conclusion is buttressed by the explicit statements of revolutionary leaders. For example, while calling for greater emphasis on moral incentives and political consciousness, Fidel Castro has continued since 1986 to call for intermediate-level personnel who have "master[ed] the science of organization and management."[32] He has touted the need for trained economic professionals to make detailed analyses of the operation of the SDPE and to assist the revolutionary leadership in correcting problems.[33] He has attacked old cadre administrators who, out of buddyism and fear for their jobs, have systematically overstaffed the administrative apparatus with their own kind and have held back the young new professionals under them.[34] And he has stated that, not seniority, which of course benefits the old cadres, but educational credentials should determine who remains and rises in intermediate-level positions.[35]

As the revolutionary leadership has called for the speedier rise of the new professionals, however, it has also called for stricter limits on them. First, Fidel Castro's critique of the 1980 General Wage Reform, mentioned above, portends, among other things, smaller pay differentials for educational credentials, and therefore stricter limits on remuneration for new professionals. Second, Castro has also blamed many of the problems of the SDPE evident after 1980 on the overenthusiasm of technocratic new professionals for "capitalist" mechanisms.[36] Third, throughout this rectification process, Fidel Castro has strongly reemphasized that economic professionals should attend to checking the results and working out the details of the operation of the SDPE, but should leave the decisions about which mechanisms to use and all other fundamental economic decisions to the revolutionary leadership itself.[37] He has also warned against the proliferation of graduate studies that are overly theoretical and not practically related to production.[38] In effect, Castro has reemphasized that the new professionals should attend to concrete details, and should refrain from questioning or attempting to appropriate the societal decisions that the revolutionary leadership continues to claim as its exclusive province.

How effective will the various policy changes wrought by the 1986 rectification process be in reducing the general level of bureaucratic centralism in Cuba? Putting this and a host of related problems at the center of political attention, as the revolutionary leadership has done, of course should help, as should the more rapid decline of the old cadres and at least some of the limits put on the rising new professionls. Greater workers' participation in discussing the basic production issues of their enterprises and work centers should also help, as presumably would something that is not on the current political agenda, namely, much more workers' participation in economic planning beyond their enterprises and work centers, in the regional and national arenas. But, through the Party, the leadership has taken on increased responsibility for economic performance at all levels in this rectification process: this perhaps portends that it is nowhere near to jettisoning its own bureaucratic centralist habits.

Ultimately, the question remains whether the Cuban attempt to reduce significantly the incidence and intensity of bureaucratic centralism will work. Will relying in large part on raising consciousness prove sufficient to counteract not only the sociohistorical but also the systemic causes of bureaucratic centralism in Cuba? This attempt, of course, sets the Cuban rectification drive since 1986 apart from recent Soviet and Eastern European reforms involving increased use of material incentives and market mechanisms. The long-term prospects for these experiments to significantly mitigate the problem of bureaucratic centralism in their respective economies remain open. But both experiments bear watching; either could have profound consequences for the future of existing socialism.

CUBAN STUDIES AND THE INTERMEDIATE LEVELS

It was argued in Chapter 1 that, even when societal decisions remain in the hands of the revolutionary leadership, nevertheless intermediate-level strata and workers commonly play an important role in the discussions that precede these decisions. Intermediate personnel often possess relevant information, knowledge, and skills and socialist workers cannot easily be limited to "economistic" demands or disciplined by the "whip of hunger." Therefore, revolutionary leaders are very likely to have to invite their participation in pre-decision-making discussions. Moreover, it was argued that in any case workers and intermediate-level personnel necessarily exert considerable influence in the post-decision-making process of implementation. Both can execute or block, expediate or delay, abide by or distort, the implementation of leadership decisions.

How have these points, which justify jettisoning the elite/mass perspective prevalent in Cuban studies, been illustrated by the analysis of this study? To answer this question, it is not necessary to repeat the whole argument of this book. Rather, what is needed is a schematic review highlighting the major insights gained by admitting intermediate actors and workers into the circle of politically relevant actors.

First, the relevance of focusing on intermediate strata became evident in examining the problem of scarce, altogether lacking, or misallocated skills that faced the early revolutionary regime. This problem was caused most directly by the deficiencies of Cuba's prerevolutionary educational system, which taught too few students, poorly taught those it did teach, and often taught them the wrong things. But the situation was considerably aggravated by the postrevolutionary exodus of relatively skilled U.S. personnel, the majority of Cuba's larger property owners, and a significant proportion, albiet a minority, of the prerevolutionary intermediate-level strata. Thus, although the early exodus of intermediate personnel did not create the country's poor skill profile, this did worsen it.

Moreover, which individuals in intermediate occupations left and who stayed would seem to have been considerably influenced by the character of the skills they possessed. Legal professionals, teachers, and others whose skills resulted in a trained incapacity to adapt to the new revolutionary society left in greater numbers. Small business proprietors who were allowed to prosper until the Revolutionary Offensive of 1968, as well as managers, executives, and others whose skills could often be easily adapted to the new revolutionary society, were much less likely to leave. While many in intermediate-level occupations suffered from official discrimination that may have motivated them eventually to join the exodus, many others rapidly moved up in the new revolutionary administrative apparatus. Thus, focusing on the intermediate level of Cuban society added to our knowledge of the country's postrevolutionary skill problem and of the social composition of the exodus that contributed to it.

Second, such a focus on the intermediate strata helped us understand the two aspects of the leadership's response to the skill problem over the first decade of the revolution. On the one hand, throughout the 1960s the leadership minimized the demand for intermediate-level skills by coopting less trained individuals into administrative positions on the basis of political rather than educational credentials. On the other hand, although the leadership had a variety of reasons for introducing the *fidelista* organizational and motivational system in the late 1960s, it did so in part out of a desire to minimize the demand for skills. The *fidelista* system shunted many incumbents of intermediate-level occupations out of their administrative offices into fields and factories, that is, directly into production. Overall, it called for fewer administrative controls and, therefore, for fewer administrative controllers. Economic controls, in particular, were eliminated or weakened, and economic professionals and their skills denigrated.

Still, the leadership actually increased the supply of skills in the 1960s by expanding all levels of Cuban education, especially primary schooling and literacy programs. Its successes in this regard were dramatic. By the end of the decade, however, certain earlier gains were being lost. This resulted in part from the impact on education of the *fidelista* system, which pulled many individuals out of adult, secondary, and higher education classes and into regular or voluntary labor. The impact of the *fidelista* downgrading of economic controls was reflected in the dramatic drop in higher education economic studies enrollments in the late 1960s. Thus, the leadership's response to the demand side of the skill problem helped shape its response to the supply side.

Third, when the crisis finally emerged in 1970, workers were among the most politically relevant actors. This crisis arose from the *fidelista* implementation of Cuba's second economic development strategy and the response to it on the part of workers. Although some workers responded as New Persons with great sacrifice and effort, others proved less than ideal implementers of the leadership's policies. Lacking effective mechanisms through which to criticize these policies or their consequences, many workers became demoralized and withdrew productive effort. As 1970 approached, the rate of absenteeism soared and productivity plummeted. The deficiencies of the *fidelista* implementation of the second development strategy manifested themselves in a variety of ways, but, ultimately, it was the noncooperation of Cuban workers that forced the revolutionary leadership to jettison the *fidelista* system and to launch the post–1970 rectification drive.

Fourth, focusing on workers and intermediate personnel aided understanding of this rectification process. In part, this drive of the 1970s involved an even more dramatic expansion of the educational system than in the 1960s. This enabled the system to decisively address the workers' skill problem, and to supply an increasing number of Cubans with at least a secondary school degree to serve as new professionals in the expanding intermediate-level occupations. The post–1970 rectification drive also for the first time systematically introduced the work-study principle throughout Cuban education. In the hope of forming new professionals with revolutionary values, the work-study principle was especially emphasized at the basic secondary, preuniversity, and higher education levels. Finally, this rectification drive led to further change in the distribution of enrollments by subject area in higher education. Especially noteworthy was the dramatic increase in economic studies enrollments, which reflected the need for a greater number of economic and other administrative professionals to operate the organizational structures introduced after 1970.

The other part of the post–1970 rectification process involved an attempt to balance the material and moral sides of the new incentive system and to institutionalize new economic and political organizations designed to operate according to democratic centralist principles for making and implementing decisions. These principles stipulated that the revolutionary leadership should retain control over societal decisions. But they also called for solidifying worker support for these decisions through various forms of participation, and for devolving greater administrative responsibilities on intermediate personnel. If these responsibilities were to be competently carried out, the old cadres who had risen to intermediate-level occupations in the 1960s on the basis of political credentials would either be displaced by or have to convert themselves into new professionals through further education. Thus, the institutionalization of the new democratic centralist system increased the demand for new professionals.

Sixth, in order to understand some of the political difficulties involved in the post–1970 rectification process, it was necessary to attend to how the leadership attempted to manage this transition from old cadres to new professionals. The old cadres were criticized for lacking skills, having bureaucratic habits, being chatterers and superexecutives, and engaging in buddyism to hide their own and their friend's incompetence and protect their positions. But, at the same time, the leadership promulgated a policy that, while favoring the rise of new professionals into intermediate occupations, attempted to relieve the old cadres' fears of being displaced by and to encourage them to convert themselves into new professionals. In general, at least up to 1986, the leadership opted for a policy of gradual transition from an administrative apparatus dominated by old cadres to one occupied by new professionals.

The leadership favored the rise of the new professionals in a variety of ways. It launched the post–1970 rectification process that greatly increased both the supply of and demand for new professionals. In addition, it promulgated policies that favored the rise of the new professionals to intermediate-level posts and remunerated them for their educational achievements. At the same time, however, the leadership attempted to limit the ability of the new professionals to seek material privileges and to debate overall societal decisions. Taking for example the economic professionals, it can be seen concretely how the new professionals have been enabled to express certain professional concerns, while their decision-making power has been limited to implementing the revolutionary leadership's decisions. So far, Cuba's leaders have effectively denied the new professionals the right to debate the larger issues of socialist development.

Seventh, many factors had to be called upon to explain why the operation of the post–1970 system was plagued, at least up to 1986, by bureaucratic centralist behavior. But focusing on intermediate-level personnel, not just leaders and workers, could help explain the high incidence and intensity of bureaucratic centralism in Cuba, and the different probabilities for the various types of actors for engaging in such behavior. For example, we have shown how Cuba's old cadres have probably been more attracted than new professionals to bureaucratic centralist behavior. As with the bureaucratic habits of the revolutionary leadership, this is explained in part as the legacy of the *fidelista* system of the late 1960s. In addition, Cuban workers were shown to have actively helped to distort the implementation of the leadership's societal decisions.

Finally, the focus on intermediate personnel and on workers has helped illuminate certain dimensions of the leadership's latest rectification effort which might otherwise have been overlooked. In part, since 1986 the leadership seems to have attempted to eliminate bureaucratic centralism by effecting a more rapid transition from the old cadres to the new professionals. It has attacked the practice of promotion by seniority that the old cadres have used to fill administrative posts with their buddies and to hold back the new professionals beneath them. The leadership has also involved workers more regularly than in the past in solving problems and in participating in discussing the basic production issues of their enterprises and work centers. As has also been seen, however, the leadership has so far shown little evidence that it is ready to limit its own bureaucratic centralist habits.

It is, of course, impossible to foretell the exact unfolding of this rectification process. However, continuing attention to the role of intermediate personnel and of workers clearly presents the most promising approach for understanding the character and direction of Cuban socialism in the years ahead. This study has only begun to probe the evolving and still dynamic Cuban reality. But this analysis has revealed formerly unrecognized complexities of Cuba's changing stratification system and of its ongoing political conflicts. If this study has accomplished its purpose, it has moved beyond elite/mass approaches to Cuban socialism, and thereby suggested a more sophisticated path of analysis for Cuban studies.

Scholars taking up this mode of analysis will find a number of interesting questions to examine. Will the old cadres find ever newer ways to resist displacement by or conversion into new professionals? Will the new professionals develop their own forms of self-protection and aggrandizement? Will the new professionals eventually revolt against the limits placed on them by revolutionary leaders, especially those restrictions that limit their ability to debate the larger issues of socialism? What will happen as the present generation of Cuban revolutionary leaders passes on? Will it be replaced by the new professionals? If so, how will these respond to the demands and expectations of Cuban workers? Will new professionals in power carry the revolution forward?

Since Cuba is just one case of many, the attempt to answer such questions should benefit from comparative research. The current ferment in the socialist world over the definition and future of socialism should provide multiple openings for the pursuit of such research. How will the current Cuban emphasis on revolutionary values and political consciousness fare in a socialist world turning increasingly to greater reliance on material incentives and market mechanisms? Will such a turn prove attractive to Cuba's new professional stratum as it grows in size, develops in confidence, and perhaps succeeds to power? Might it be that the transition from old cadres to new professionals which this study has uncovered in Cuba is simply a later historical version of what has already taken place in many other socialist countries? Are what we see in Cuba today and in the rest of the socialist world various stages of the formation of a ''new class'' within the revolutionary process?

This book cannot provide the answers to these questions. A yes, of course, would add steam to the various theories, cited in Chapter 1, that view the intermediate stratum in socialist societies as a rising new class. A no, on the other hand, would sustain the Marxian hope for a participatory, egalitarian, and just world. But whichever proves correct in the long run, understanding the process by which socialism moves into the future, in Cuba and elsewhere, means going beyond stale elite/mass approaches toward more sophisticated perspectives that widen the focus of analytic attention to encompass the dynamics of the intermediate level of socialist society.

NOTES

1. ''Report on Fidel Castro's Closing Remarks at the 53rd Plenary Meeting of the National Council of the Central Organization of Cuban Trade Unions,'' *Granma Weekly Review*, Feb. 1, 1987, pp. 2–4.

2. This, at least, is the reasonable conclusion to draw from Fidel Castro's insistence that Cuba could not expect to solve its economic problems with further

assistance from the socialist countries, but instead had to improve the overall efficiency of its economy. See "Report on Fidel Castro's Closing Remarks at the Meeting of the Provincial Committee of the Party," *Granma Weekly Review*, Jan. 25, 1987, p. 2.

3. "Report on Fidel Castro's Closing Remarks at the 53rd Plenary," pp. 2–4.

4. For a brief overview of Cuba's economic problems, see Fidel Castro, "Speech to the 3rd Congress of the Committees for the Defense of the Revolution," *Granma Weekly Review*, Oct. 12, 1986, p. 3.

5. For example, it was recognized that the provision of housing was falling behind need more rapidly than before, especially in the city of Havana. In addition, for the first time since the revolutionary triumph of 1959, the infant mortality rate rose in 1985. See *Granma Weekly Review*, Feb. 1, 1987, p. 1.

6. See the remarks of José M. Acosta at the "Meeting of Basic Industry Enterprise Directors," *Granma Weekly Review*, Feb. 15, 1987, pp. 4–5.

7. "Report on Fidel Castro's Closing Remarks at the 53rd Plenary," p. 2; and his remarks in "Debates on Rectification of Errors and Negative Tendencies in Various Spheres of Society at the Deferred Session of the Third Congress of the Communist Party of Cuba," *Granma Weekly Review*, Dec. 4, 1986, p. 2.

8. "Report on Fidel Castro's Closing Remarks at the 53rd Plenary," p. 4.

9. Fidel Castro, "Speech to the 3rd Congress," Oct. 12, 1986, p. 4.

10. "Report on Fidel Castro's Closing Remarks at the 53rd Plenary," p. 2.

11. "Report on Fidel Castro's Closing Remarks at the Meeting of the Provincial Committee," p. 2.

12. "Report on Fidel Castro's Closing Remarks at the 53rd Plenary," p. 2.

13. Fidel Castro, "Closing Speech at the 2nd National Meeting of Agricultural Production Cooperatives," *Granma Weekly Review*, June 1, 1986, pp. 3–4. In the same speech, Castro also claimed that, since these markets accounted for only 2 percent of the total value of marketed food in 1986, the gap created by their abolition would be filled by state supplies to the parallel market.

14. "Report on Fidel Castro's Analysis of the Economic Situation and the Essential Measures to Be Taken," *Granma Weekly Review*, Jan. 11, 1987, pp. 2–5.

15. "Report on Fidel Castro's Closing Remarks at the 53rd Plenary," p. 4.

16. Ibid., p. 2.

17. "Report on Fidel Castro's Closing Remarks at the Provincial Committee," p. 4.

18. "Report on Fidel Castro's Closing Remarks at the 53rd Plenary," p. 4.

19. Ibid., p. 2.

20. Fidel Castro, "Speech to the 3rd Congress," p. 4; "Report on Fidel Castro's Analysis of the Economic Situation," p. 4.

21. "Report on Fidel Castro's Closing Remarks at the Provincial Committee," p. 2.

22. "National Meeting of Party's Economic Departments", *Granma Weekly Review*, Feb. 15, 1987, p. 1.

23. *Granma Weekly Review*, July 6, 1986, p. 2.

24. "Report on Fidel Castro's Speech at the Opening of the Julio Trigo Hospital", *Granma Weekly Review*, Sept. 20, 1987, p. 4.

25. Fidel Castro, "Speech at the Close of the Deferred Session of the Third Congress of the Communist Party of Cuba," *Granma Weekly Review*, Dec. 14, 1986, p. 13.

26. "Report on Fidel Castro's Speech at the 25th Anniversary of the Proclamation of the Socialist Nature of the Revolution and the Victory at Playa Giron," *Granma Weekly Review*, April 27, 1986, p. 10.

27. Fidel Castro, "Closing Speech at the 2nd National Meeting," p. 4.

28. "Report on Fidel Castro's Closing Remarks at the 53rd Plenary Meeting," p. 4.

29. José A. López Moreno, "Report on the Fulfillment of the 1985 Plan for Economic and Social Development and the Objectives Set for 1986," *Granma Weekly Review*, Jan. 12, 1986, p. 4.

30. In 1981, 19 such brigades were introduced in the agricultural sector. By 1986, their number had grown to 2,055. See Cino Colina, "The New Type Brigades," *Granma Weekly Review*, Feb. 9, 1986, p. 5.

31. "Debates on Rectification of Errors," pp. 8–9.

32. "Report on Fidel Castro's Remarks at the 2nd Meeting of Havana Enterprises," *Granma Weekly Review*, July 5, 1987, p. 5.

33. Ibid.

34. "5th Congress of the Communist Youth League (UJC)," *Granma Weekly Review*, April 12, 1987, p. 5; and see also the "Deferred Session of the 5th Central Committee Plenum," *Granma Weekly Review*, Oct. 4, 1987, p. 5. Although Castro pointed directly to such practices in the agricultural sector, the study of the Nicaro Nickel plant, which revealed that, of its 184 engineers, only 6 percent were utilized in "a satisfactory manner," 70 percent were "under-utilized," and the rest were "poorly" used, probably indicates that such practices are widespread in industry as well. See "Meeting of the Enterprise Directors of the Ministry of Basic Industry," *Granma Weekly Review*, Feb. 15, 1987, p. 5.

35. Fidel Castro, "Speech at the Main Ceremony to Commemorate the 35th Anniversary of the Attack on Moncada," *Granma Weekly Review*, Aug. 7, 1988, pp. 2–5.

36. Ibid.; and *Granma Weekly Review*, July 6, 1986, p. 2.

37. "Report on Fidel Castro's Remarks at the 2nd Meeting," p. 5.

38. "Meeting of the Enterprise Directors," p. 5.

Bibliography

CUBAN PERIODICALS

Bohemia

Cuba Socialista

Cuestiones de la Economía Planificada

Economía y Desarrollo

Educación

Granma

Granma Weekly Review

Revista Cubana de Derecho

Sobre Educación Superior

Trabajadores

Universidad de la Habana

OFFICIAL CUBAN DOCUMENTS

Asociación Nacional de Economistas de Cuba. ''Constitución.'' *Economía y Desarrollo* 52 (Mar.-Apr. 1979): 24–83.

Comité Estatal de Estadísticos. *Compendio anuario estadístico de la Republica de Cuba, 1976*. Cuba: 1976.

Comité Estatal de Estadísticas, Dirección de Demografía. *Encuesta demografía nacional de 1979—metodología y tablas seleccionades*. Havana: 1981.

————. *Encuesta demografía nacional de 1979: principales características laborales de la población de Cuba*. Havana: 1981.

Consejo Superior de Universidades. *La reforma de la enseñanza superior en Cuba*. Havana: 1962.

Constitution of the Republic of Cuba. New York: Center for Cuban Studies, 1976.

Federación de Mujeres Cubanas. *Cuban Women in Higher Education*. Havana: Editorial Letras Cubanas, 1985.

Junta Central de Planificación. *Segunda plenaria nacional de chequeo de la implantación del SDPE*. Havana: Ediciones JUCEPLAN, 1980.

"Ley que crea el Ministerio de Educación Superior." *Universidad de la Habana*, nos. 203/204 (1976): 171–75.

Memoirs: Second Congress of the Association of Third World Economists. Havana: Editorial de Ciéncias Sociales, 1982.

Memorias del XIII Congreso de la CTC. Havana: 1973.

Ministerio de Educación. *Cuba: organización de la educación, 1981–1983, informe a la XXXIX Conferencia Internacional de Educación, Genebra, Suiza*. Havana, 1984.

————. *Documentos directivas para el perfeccionamiento del Sistema Nacional de Educación*. Cuba: 1975.

————. *Informe a la Asamblea Nacional del Poder Popular*. Havana: 1981.

————. *Informe de la delegacion de la Republica de Cuba a la VII Conferencia de Ministros de Educación Superior y Media Especializada de los Países Socialistas*. Havana: 1972.

————. *El plan de perfeccionamiento y desarrollo del Sistema Nacional de Educación de Cuba*. Havana: 1976.

————. *El principio de la combinación del trabajo en la educación superior: Informe a la conferencia de ministros de educación superior de países socialistas*. Havana: 1974.

Oficina Nacional de los Censos Demográfica y Electora. *Censos de población, viviendos y electoral*. Havana: 1953.

Primer Congreso del Partido Comunista de Cuba. *Tesis y resoluciones*. Havana: Editorial de Ciéncias Sociales, 1978.

Reglamento de las Asambleas Nacional, Provincial, y Municipal del Poder Popular. Havana: Editorial Obre, 1979.

Second Congress of the Communist Party of Cuba. *Documents and Speeches*. Havana: Political Publishers, 1981.

Segunda plenaria nacional de chequeo de la implantación del SDPE. Havana: Ediciones JUCEPLAN, 1980.

Sistema de arbitraje estatal y normas básicas para los contratos económicos. Havana: Editorial Obre, 1978.

BOOKS, PAMPHLETS, AND ARTICLES

Arendt, Hannah. *The Origins of Totalitarianism*. New York: Harcourt Brace, 1966.

Bach, Robert L. "The New Cuban Immigrants: Their Background and Prospects." In U.S. House of Representatives, Committee on the Judiciary, *Caribbean Migration*, 96th Congress, 1980.

Bach, Robert L., et al. "The Flotilla 'Entrants': Latest and Most Controversial." *Cuban Studies/Estudios Cubanos* 11/12 (July 1981-Jan. 1982): 29–48.

Barghoorn, Frederick. *Politics in the USSR*. 2nd ed. Boston: Little, Brown, 1972.

Barzun, Jacques, and Henry F. Graff. *The Modern Researcher*. 3rd ed. New York: Harcourt Brace Jovanovich, 1977.

Bauman, Zygmunt. "Social Dissent in the East European Political System." *Archives Europeénes de Sociologie* 12 (1971): 25–51.

Bengelsdorf, Carollee. "A Large School of Government." *Cuba Review* 6, no. 3 (Sept. 1976): 6–18.

Benjamin, Medea, et al. *No Free Lunch: Food and Revolution in Cuba Today*. San Francisco: Institute for Food and Development Policy, 1984.

Betto, Frei. *Fidel on Religion*. Sydney, Australia: Pathfinder Press, 1986.

Bonachea, Rolando, and Nelson Valdés, eds. *Cuba in Revolution*. Garden City, New York: Doubleday, 1972.

Boorstein, Edward. *The Economic Transformation of Cuba*. New York: Monthly Review Press, 1968.

Bray, Donald W., and Timothy F. Harding. "Cuba." In Ronald H. Chilcote and Joel C. Edelstein, eds., *Latin America: The Struggle with Dependency and Beyond*, 579–734. Cambridge, Massachusetts: Schenkman Publishing, 1974.

Brundenius, Claes. *Economic Growth, Basic Needs and Income Distribution in Revolutionary Cuba*. Lund, Sweden: University of Lund, 1981.

———. *Revolutionary Cuba: The Challenge of Economic Growth with Equity*. Boulder, Colorado: Westview Press, 1984.

———. "Some Notes on the Development of the Cuban Labor Force 1979–80." *Cuban Studies/Estudios Cubanos* 13, no. 2 (Summer 1983): 65–77.

Brunner, Heinrich. *Cuban Sugar Policy from 1963 to 1970*. Pittsburgh: University of Pittsburgh Press, 1977.

Brzezinski, Zbigniew, and Carl G. Friedrich. *Totalitarian Dictatorship and Autocracy*. New York: Praeger, 1956.

Bukharin, Nikolai. *The Economics of the Transformation Period*. New York: Bergman, 1971.

Casal, Lourdes. "Cuban Communist Party: The Best among the Good." *Cuba Review* 6, no. 3 (Sept. 1976): 24–27.

———. "On Popular Power: The Organization of the Cuban State during the Period of Transition." *Latin American Perspectives*, Supplement 1975, pp. 78–88.

Castro, Fidel. *Fidel in Chile*. New York: International Publishers, 1975.

———. *Main Report to the First Congress of the Communist Party of Cuba*. Havana: Communist Party of Cuba, 1977.

————. *We Were Born to Overcome, Not to Be Overrun*. (Havana: Editorial Política, 1984).

————. *The World Economic and Social Crisis*. Havana: The Council of State, 1983.

CEPAL. *Cuba: estilo de desarrollo y políticos sociales*. Cerro del Agua, México: Siglo Veintiuno Editores, 1980.

Chilcote, Ronald H., and Joel C. Edelstein, eds. *Latin America: The Struggle with Dependency and Beyond*. Cambridge: Schenkman Publishing, 1974.

Cockburn, Cynthia. "People's Power." In John Griffiths and Peter Griffiths, eds., *Cuba: The Second Decade*, 18–35. London: Writers and Readers Publishing Cooperative, 1979.

Corona Zayas, Enrique. *Los contratos económicos y el arbitraje en la legislación de SDPE*. Havana: Centro de Información Científico Técnica de JU-CEPLAN, 1979.

"Cuba's New 'Free Market.'" *Cuba Update* 1, no. 3 (Sept. 1980): 1–2.

Demographic Yearbook, Historical Supplement. New York: United Nations Organization, 1979.

Díaz-Briquets, Sergio, and Lisandro Pérez. *Cuba: The Demography of Revolution*. Washington, D.C.: The Population Reference Bureau, 1981.

Dingwall, Robert, and Philip Lewis, eds. *The Sociology of the Professions*. London: Macmillan, 1983.

Domínguez, Jorge. *Cuba: Order and Revolution*. Cambridge: Harvard University Press, 1978.

————. "Institutionalization and Civil-Military Relations in Cuba." *Cuban Studies/Estudios Cubanos* 6 (Jan. 1976): 39–65.

Dorticós, Osvaldo. *Discurso en el acto de presentación de los militantes del Partido del Instituto de Economía*. Havana: Editorial de Ciéncias Sociales, 1969.

Dumont, René. *Cuba: Est-il Socialiste?* Paris: Éditions du Seuil, 1970.

Fagen, Richard. *The Transformation of Political Culture in Cuba*. Stanford: Stanford University Press, 1969.

Fagen, Richard, et al. *Cubans in Exile: Disaffection and Revolution*. Stanford: Stanford University Press, 1968.

Fallenbucki, Zbigniew M., ed. *Economic Development in the Soviet Union and Eastern Europe*. Vol 1. New York: Praeger, 1975.

Ferreira Báez, Francisco. "El sistema de formación profesional de nivel medio en Cuba." In Haydée García and Hans Blumenthal, eds., *Formación profesional en Latinoamerica*, 111–38. Caracas: Editorial Nueva Sociedad, 1987.

Figueroa, Max, et al. *The Basic Secondary School in the Countryside: An Educational Innovation in Cuba*. Paris: UNESCO, 1974.

Fitzgerald, Frank T. "A Critique of the 'Sovietization of Cuba' Thesis." *Science and Society* 42 (Spring 1978): 1–32.

————. "Cuba and the Problem of Socialist Development." *Monthly Review* 33, no. 11 (April 1982): 48–51.

———. "The 'Sovietization of Cuba Thesis' Revisted." In Andrew Zimbalist, ed., *Cuban Political Economy: Controversies in Cubanology*, 137–53. Boulder, Colorado: Westview Press, 1988; and in *Science and Society* 51, no. 4 (Winter 1987–1988): 439–57.

Friedgut, Theodore. "Interests and Groups in Soviet Policy-Making: The MTS Reforms." *Soviet Studies* 28 (Oct. 1976): 524–47.

Friedrich, Carl G., et al. *Totalitarianism in Perspective*. New York: Praeger, 1969.

Friedrich, Carl G., and Zbigniew Brzezinski. *Totalitarian Dictatorship and Autocracy*. New York: Praeger, 1956.

Friedson, Eliot. "The Theory of Professions: State of the Art." In Robert Dingwall and Philip Lewis, eds., *The Sociology of the Professions*, 19–37. London: Macmillan, 1983.

Fuller, Linda. "Changes in the Relationship among Unions, Administration, and the Party at the Cuban Workplace, 1959–1982." *Latin American Perspectives* 13, no. 2 (Spring 1986): 6–32.

García, Concepción, and Eugene F. Provenzano. "Exiled Teachers and the Cuban Revolution." *Cuban Studies/Estudios Cubanos* 13, no. 1 (Winter 1983): 1–15.

García, Haydée, and Hans Blumenthal, eds. *Formación profesional en Latinoamerica*. Caracas: Editorial Nueva Sociedad, 1987.

Gerassi, John, ed. *Venceremos! The Speeches and Writings of Che Guevara*. New York: Simon and Schuster, 1968.

Gerth, Hans, and C. Wright Mills, eds. *From Max Weber: Essays in Sociology*. New York: Oxford University Press, 1958.

Giddens, Anthony. *The Class Structure of Advanced Societies*. Rev. ed. New York: Harper and Row, 1981.

González, Edward. "Castro and Cuba's New Orthodoxy." *Problems of Communism* 25 (Jan.-Feb. 1976): 1–19.

———. "Complexities of Cuban Foreign Policy." *Problems of Communism* 26 (Nov.-Dec. 1977): 1–15.

———. "Political Succession in Cuba." *Studies in Comparative Communism* 9 (Spring/Summer 1976): 80–107.

Gouldner, Alvin. *The Future of the Intellectuals and the Rise of the New Class*. New York: Seabury Press, 1979.

Graff, Henry F., and Jacques Barzun. *The Modern Researcher*. 3rd ed. New York: Harcourt Brace Jovanovich, 1977.

Griffiths, Franklin, and H. Gordon Skilling. *Interest Groups in Soviet Politics*. Princeton, New Jersey: Princeton University Press, 1971.

Griffiths, John, and Peter Griffiths, eds. *Cuba: The Second Decade*. London: Writers and Readers Publishing Cooperative, 1979.

Halebsky, Sandor, and John M. Kirk, eds. *Cuba: Twenty-Five Years of Revolution*. New York: Praeger, 1985.

Harneker, Marta. *Cuba: Dictatorship or Democracy?* Westport, Connecticut: Lawrence Hill, 1980.

Herrara, Antonio José, and Hernan Rosenkranz. "Political Consciousness in Cuba." In John Griffiths and Peter Griffiths, eds., *Cuba: The Second Decade*, 36–52. London: Writers and Readers Cooperative, 1979.

Huberman, Leo, and Paul Sweezy. *Socialism in Cuba*. New York: Monthly Review Press, 1969.

Huteau, Michel, and Jacques Lautrey. *L'Éducation à Cuba*. Paris: François Maspero, 1973.

"Interview with José R. Fernández, Minister of Education." *Cuba Update* 1, no. 6 (Jan. 1981): 3.

Karol, K. S. *Guerrillas in Power: The Course of the Cuban Revolution*. New York: Hill and Wang, 1970.

Keech, William R., and Joel J. Schwartz. "Group Influence and the Policy Process in the Soviet Union." *American Political Science Review* 3 (Sept. 1968): 840–51.

Kenner, Martin, and James Petras, eds. *Fidel Castro Speaks*. New York: Grove Press, 1969.

Kolesnikov, Nikolai. *Cuba educación popular y preparación de los cuadros nacionales, 1959–1982*. Moscow: Editorial Progreso. 1983.

Konrad, George, and Ivan Szelenyi. *The Intellectuals on the Road to Class Power*. New York: Harcourt Brace Jovanovich, 1979.

Kornai, Janos. *Contradictions and Dilemmas*. Cambridge: Massachusetts Institute of Technology, 1986.

———. *Economics of Shortage*. Amsterdam: North-Holland, 1980.

Lane, David. "Marxist Class Conflict Analysis of State Socialist Society." In Richard Scase, ed., *Industrial Society: Class, Cleavage and Control*, 172–90. New York: St. Martin's Press, 1977.

———. *The Socialist Industrial State*. Boulder, Colorado: Westview Press, 1976.

———, and Felicity O'Dell. *The Soviet Industrial Worker*. New York: St. Martin's Press, 1978.

Leiner, Marvin. *Children Are the Revolution*. New York: Penguin Books, 1978.

———. "Cuba's Schools: 25 Years Later." In Sandor Halebsky and John M. Kirk, eds., *Cuba: Twenty-Five Years of Revolution*, 27–44. New York: Praeger, 1985.

LeoGrande, William M. "Continuity and Change in the Cuban Political Elite." *Cuban Studies/Estudios Cubanos* 8 (July 1978): 1–31.

León, Laureano. "Hacia la eficacia económica." *America Latina* (January 1989): 4–9.

Lewis, Phillip, and Robert Dingwall, eds. *The Sociology of the Professions*. London: Macmillan, 1983.

Lockwood, Lee. *Castro's Cuba, Cuba's Fidel*. New York: Vintage Books, 1969.

London, Kurt, ed. *The Soviet Union: A Half-Century of Communism*. Baltimore: Johns Hopkins Press, 1968.

Luxemburg, Rosa. "What Is Economics?" In Mary-Alice Waters, ed., *Rosa Luxemburg Speaks*, 219–45. New York: Pathfinder Press, 1970.

MacEwan, Arthur. "Incentives, Equality, and Power in Revolutionary Cuba." In Ronald Radosh, ed., *The New Cuba*, 74–101. New York: Morrow, 1976.

———. *Revolution and Economic Development in Cuba*. New York: St. Martin's Press, 1981.

Martel, Raúl. *La empresa socialista*. Havana: Editorial de Ciéncias Sociales, 1979.

Martínez Heredia, Fernando. *Rectificación y profundización del socialismo en Cuba*. Buenos Aires: Ediciones Dialéctica, 1989.

McAuley, Mary. *Politics and the Soviet Union*. New York: Penguin, 1977.

Mesa-Lago, Carmelo. *Cuba in the 1970s: Pragmatism and Institutionalization*. Albuquerque: University of New Mexico Press, 1974.

———. "Economic Significance of Unpaid Labor in Socialist Cuba." *Industrial and Labor Relations Review* 22 (April 1969): 339–57.

———. *The Economy of Socialist Cuba*. Albuquerque: University of New Mexico Press, 1981.

———. *The Labor Force, Employment, Unemployment and Underemployment in Cuba: 1899–1970*. Beverly Hills, California: Sage Publications, 1972.

"New Hero: Whistle-Blower Silvia Marjorie Spence." *Cuba Update* 8, no. 1–2 (Spring 1987): 7.

O'Connor, Walter D. *Public Opinion in European Socialist Systems*. New York: Praeger, 1977.

———. "Social Consequences of Economic Reform in Eastern Europe." In Zbigniew M. Fallenbucki, ed., *Economic Development in the Soviet Union and Eastern Europe*, Vol. 1, 65–99. New York: Praeger, 1975.

O'Dell, Felicity, and David Lane. *The Soviet Industrial Worker*. New York: St. Martin's Press, 1978.

Parkin, Frank. "System Contradiction and Political Transformation." *Archives Europeénes de Sociologie* 13 (1972): 45–62.

Parry, Albert. *The New Class Divided: Science and Technology versus Communism*. New York: Macmillan, 1966.

Pérez, Humberto. *Sobre las dificultades objetivas de la revolución: lo que el pueblo deber saber*. Havana: Editorial Política, 1979.

Pérez-Stable, Marifeli, "Institutionalization and the Workers' Response." *Cuban Studies/Estudios Cubanos* 6, no. 2 (July 1976): 31–54.

———. "Whither the Cuban Working Class?" *Latin American Perspectives*, Supplement 1975, pp. 60–77.

Portes, Alejandro, et al. "The New Wave: A Statistical Profile of Recent Cuban Exiles to the United States." *Cuban Studies/Estudios Cubanos* 7, no. 1 (Jan. 1977): 1–32.

Provenzano, Eugene F., and Concepción García. "Exiled Teachers and the Cuban Revolution." *Cuban Studies/Estudios Cubanos* 13, no. 1 (Winter 1983): 1–15.

Radosh, Ronald, ed. *The New Cuba*. New York: Morrow, 1976.

Rafael Rodríguez, Carlos. *Palabras en los setenta*. Havana: Editorial de Ciéncias Sociales, 1984.

Rakovsky, Marc. *Towards an East European Marxism*. New York: St. Martin's Press, 1978.

Ritter, Archibald R. M. *The Economic Development of Revolutionary Cuba*. New York: Praeger, 1974.

————. "The Organs of People's Power and the Communist Party: The Nature of Cuban Democracy." In Sandor Halebsky and John M. Kirk, eds., *Cuba: Twenty-Five Years of Revolution*, 270–90. New York: Praeger, 1985.

Roca, Sergio. "State Enterprises in Cuba under the New System of Planning and Management (SDPE)." *Cuban Studies/Estudios Cubanos* 16 (1986): 153–79.

Seers, Dudley, ed. *Cuba: The Economic and Social Revolution*. Chapel Hill: University of North Carolina Press, 1964.

Silverman, Bertram, ed. *Man and Socialism in Cuba: The Great Debate*. New York: Atheneum, 1973.

Skilling, H. Gordon. "The Party, Opposition and Interest Groups in Communist Politics." In Kurt London, ed., *The Soviet Union: A Half-Century of Communism*, 119–49. Baltimore: Johns Hopkins Press, 1968.

————, and Franklin Griffiths. *Interest Groups in Soviet Politics*. Princeton: Princeton University Press, 1971.

Stewart, Phillip. "Soviet Interest Groups and the Policy Process: The Repeal of Production Education." *World Politics* 1 (Oct. 1969): 29–50.

Suchlicki, Jaime. *University Students and Revolution in Cuba, 1920–1968*. Coral Gables: University of Miami Press, 1968.

Taber, Michael, ed. *Fidel Castro Speeches, Vol. 2: Our Power Is that of the Working People*. New York: Pathfinder Press, 1983.

Tablada, Carlos. *Che Guevara: Economics and Politics in the Transition to Socialism*. Sydney, Australia: Pathfinder/Pacific and Asia, 1989.

"Teaching Staff Improvements." *Cuba Update* 1, no. 6 (Jan. 1981): 12.

Thomas, Hugh. *Cuba: The Pursuit of Freedom*. New York: Harper and Row, 1971.

Truman, David. *The Governmental Process*. New York: Knopf, 1971.

UNCTAD. *Health and Education Technology in Cuba*. New York: United Nations Organization, 1979.

Valdés, Nelson P. *Cuba: socialismo democrático o bureaucratismo collectivista*. Bogotá: Ediciones Tercer Mundo, 1973.

————. "The Cuban Revolution: Economic Organization and Bureaucracy." *Latin American Perspectives*, issue 20 (Winter 1979): 13–37.

Vellinga, M. L. "The Military and the Dynamics of the Cuban Revolution." *Comparative Politics* 8 (Jan. 1976): 245–71.

Wald, Karen. *Children of Che*. Palo Alto, California: Ramparts Press, 1978.

Waters, Mary-Alice, ed. *Rosa Luxemburg Speaks*. New York: Pathfinder Press, 1970.

Weber, Max. "Bureaucracy." In Hans Gerth and C. Wright Mills, eds., *From Max Weber: Essays in Sociology*, 196–244. New York: Oxford University Press, 1958.

White, Stephen. "Contradiction and Change in State Socialism." *Soviet Studies* 26 (Jan. 1974): 41–55.

Zeitlin, Maurice. *Revolutionary Politics and the Cuban Working Class*. Princeton, New Jersey: Princeton University Press, 1967.

Zimbalist, Andrew. "Cuban Economic Planning: Organization and Performance." In Sandor Halebsky and John M. Kirk, eds., *Cuba: Twenty-Five Years of Revolution*, 213–30. New York: Praeger, 1985.

————. "Workers' Participation in Cuba." *Challenge* (Nov.-Dec. 1975): 45–54.

————, ed. *Cuban Political Economy: Controversies in Cubanology*. Boulder, Colorado: Westview Press, 1988.

DISSERTATIONS

Bengelsdorf, Carollee. "Between Vision and Reality: Democracy in Socialist Theory and Practice." Massachusetts Institute of Technology, 1985.

Clark, Juan M. "The Exodus from Revolutionary Cuba (1959–1974): A Sociological Analysis." University of Florida, 1975.

Fitzgerald, Frank T. "Politics and Social Structure in Revolutionary Cuba: From the Demise of the Old Middle Class to the Rise of the New Professionals." State University of New York at Binghamton, 1985.

Fuller, Linda. "The Politics of Workers' Control in Cuba, 1959–1983: The Work Center and the National Arena." University of California at Berkeley, 1985.

Morley, Morris. "Toward a Theory of Imperial Politics: United States Policy and the Processes of State Formation, Disintegration and Consolidation in Cuba, 1898–1978." State University of New York at Binghamton, 1980.

Pérez-Stable, Marifeli. "Politics and Conciencia in Revolutionary Cuba, 1959–1984." State University of New York at Stony Brook, 1985.

Index

anti-bureaucratic revolution, 47–48, 52
auto-finance system, 43–44

bureaucratic centralism, 60–61; differential involvement of old cadres and new professionals, 123–25; of Fidel Castro, 112–13; between managers and workers, 116–21; of ministries, 113–16; systemic causes, 121–23; Types I and II defined, 111–12; within OPP, 125 n.2

Castro, Fidel: bureaucratic centralism of, 112–13; on Escalante affairs, 16 n.23; on labor hoarding, 119; on labor market, 128 n.24; on managerial competition for best workers, 117; on new professionals' seeking privileges, 100; on promotion by seniority, 92; on rectification (1986), 134–39; on technical and vocational schools, 86 n.59; on tensions among workers in late 1960s, 51; on Type I bureaucratic centralism, 126 n.16
Castro Raúl: on buddyism, 91; on lack of administrative initiative, 122–23; on

misuse of work norms, 118–19; on Party and OPP, 68–69
centralized budgetary system, 44–45
Communist Party: domination of OPP decisions, 68–69; and labor unions after 1970, 62; in rectification (1986), 136, 138, 140; role in late 1960s, 46, 52
corruption, 115; 127 nn. 19, 20
Cuban studies: elite/mass perspective in, 1–3; and interest group analysis, 3–6; new direction for, 6–9, 140–45
Cuestiones de la Economía Planificada, 102

democratic centralism: decision-making process, 60–61; organizational forms, 61–69
discrimination against intermediate-level personnel, 30–31, 46–48
Domínguez, Jorge, 2–3
Dorticós, Osvaldo: on attitude toward administrative training in 1960s, 42–43; on need for professionals, 64–65

Economía y Desarrollo, 101–2, 105
economic development strategies, 35–36, 37, 38, 59

ABOUT THE AUTHOR

FRANK T. FITZGERALD comes from a working-class family in Chicago. His mother toiled in a factory for many years. His father was troubled by a common illness that, because of poor, working-class health care, became a serious and life-long disability. Dr. Fitzgerald's concern with oppression and the possibility of its elimination through socialism grew from this background, from his own experiences in a variety of factory and office jobs, and from the movements of the 1960s. Since early in that decade, he has been active in many trade union, civil rights, peace, and international solidarity struggles.

Dr. Fitzgerald has conducted research in several Latin American countries. Most recently, he has interviewed public sector professionals in Argentina about the political and economic crisis in that country. His scholarly work has appeared in several edited volumes, and in *Monthly Review, Science and Society, Critical Sociology, Economic Forum*, the *Journal of Contemporary Asia, Cuban Studies/Estudios Cubanos, NACLA Report on the Americas, Latin American Perspectives*, and the *Journal of Latin American Studies*.

Dr. Fitzgerald is Associate Professor of Sociology at the College of Saint Rose in Albany, New York. He holds a B.S. in philosophy from Loyola University in Chicago, an M.A. in sociology from the New School for Social Research in New York City, and a Ph.D. in sociology from the State University of New York at Binghamton.